Insights You Need from
Harvard
Business
Review

GENERATIVE AI

Insights You Need from Harvard Business Review

Business is changing. Will you adapt or be left behind?

Get up to speed and deepen your understanding of the topics that are shaping your company's future with the **Insights You Need from Harvard Business Review** series. Featuring HBR's smartest thinking on fast-moving issues—blockchain, cybersecurity, AI, and more—each book provides the foundation introduction and practical case studies your organization needs to compete today and collects the best research, interviews, and analysis to get it ready for tomorrow.

You can't afford to ignore how these issues will transform the landscape of business and society. The Insights You Need series will help you grasp these critical ideas—and prepare you and your company for the future.

Books in the series include:

Agile

Artificial Intelligence

Blockchain

Climate Change

Crypto

Customer Data and Privacy

Cybersecurity

The Future of Work

Generative AI

Global Recession

Hybrid Workplace

Monopolies and Tech Giants

Multigenerational Workplace

Racial Justice

Strategic Analytics

Supply Chain

Web3

The Year in Tech 2023

The Year in Tech 2024

Insights You Need from
**Harvard
Business
Review**

GENERATIVE AI

Harvard Business Review Press
Boston, Massachusetts

Copyright 2024 Harvard Business School Publishing Corporation

All rights reserved
Printed in the United States of America

10 9 8 7 6 5 4 3 2 1

No part of this publication may be reproduced, stored in or introduced into a retrieval system, or transmitted, in any form, or by any means (electronic, mechanical, photocopying, recording, or otherwise), without the prior permission of the publisher. Requests for permission should be directed to permissions@harvardbusiness.org, or mailed to Permissions, Harvard Business School Publishing, 60 Harvard Way, Boston, Massachusetts 02163.

The web addresses referenced in this book were live and correct at the time of the book's publication but may be subject to change.

Library of Congress Cataloging-in-Publication Data

Names: Harvard Business Review Press, issuing body.
Title: Generative AI.
Other titles: Generative AI (Harvard Business Review Press) |
    Insights you need from Harvard Business Review.
Description: Boston, Massachusetts : Harvard Business Review Press,
    [2023] | Series: Insights you need series | Includes index.
Identifiers: LCCN 2023029121 (print) | LCCN 2023029122 (ebook) |
    ISBN 9781647826390 (paperback) | ISBN 9781647826406 (epub)
Subjects: LCSH: Artificial intelligence. | Business—Data processing. |
    Success in business. | Industrial management.
Classification: LCC HD30.2 .G44 2023 (print) | LCC HD30.2 (ebook) |
    DDC 658.4/0380285—dc23/eng/20230925
LC record available at https://lccn.loc.gov/2023029121
LC ebook record available at https://lccn.loc.gov/2023029122

ISBN: 978-1-64782-639-0
eISBN: 978-1-64780-640-6

The paper used in this publication meets the requirements of the American National Standard for Permanence of Paper for Publications and Documents in Libraries and Archives Z39.48-1992.

Contents

Contents

GENERATIVE AI

GENERATIVE AI WILL CHANGE YOUR BUSINESS. HERE'S HOW TO ADAPT

by David C. Edelman and Mark Abraham

t's coming. Generative AI will change the nature of how we interact with all software. And given how many brands have significant software components in how they interact with customers, generative AI will drive and distinguish how more brands compete.

In a previous HBR piece, we discussed how the use of one's customer information is already differentiating branded experiences.[1] Now, with generative AI, personalization will go even further, tailoring all aspects of digital interaction to how the customer wants it to flow, not how product designers envision cramming in more menus and features. As the software follows the customer, it will go to places that range beyond the tight boundaries of a brand's product. You will need to offer solutions to things the customer wants to do. Solve the full package of what they need and help them through their full journey to get there, even if it means linking to outside partners, rethinking the definition of your offerings, and developing the underlying data and tech architecture to connect everything involved in the solution.

Generative AI can create—generate—text, speech, images, music, video, and especially code. When that capability is joined with a feed of a person's own information and used to tailor the when, what, and how of an interaction, then the ease with which that person can get things done and the broadening accessibility of software goes up dramatically. The simple input question box that stands at the center of Google—and now of most generative AI systems, such as in ChatGPT and DALL-E 2—will power more systems. Say goodbye to software drop-down menus and the inherently guided restrictions they place on how you use them. Instead, you'll just see "What do you want to do today?" And when you type in your answer, the software will likely offer some suggestions, drawing on its knowledge of what you did last time, what your triggers are in your current context, and what you've already stored in the system as your core goals; for example, "save for a trip," "remodel our kitchen," "manage meal plans for my family of five with special dietary needs."

Without the boundaries of a conventional software interface, consumers won't care whether the brand behind the software has limitations. The change in how we interact and what we expect will be dramatic—and dramatically more democratizing.

So much of the hype on generative AI has focused on its ability to generate text, images, and sounds, but it also can create code to automate actions and facilitate pulling in external and internal data. By generating code in response to a command, it creates a shortcut that takes a user from a command to an action that simply gets the job done. Even questions about and analyses of the data stored in an application (e.g., "Who are the contacts I have not called in the last 90 days?" or "When is the next time I am scheduled to be in NYC with an opening for dinner?") will be easily handled. To answer such questions now, we have to go into an application and gather data (possibly manually) from outside of the application itself. Now the query can be recognized, code created, possibilities ranked, and the best answer generated. In milliseconds.

This drastically simplifies how we interact with what we think of as today's applications. It also enables more brands to build applications as part of their value proposition: "Given the weather, traffic, and who I'm with, give me a tourist itinerary for the afternoon, with an ongoing guide, and the ability to just buy any tickets in advance to skip any lines." "Here's my budget, here are five pictures of my current bathroom, here's what I want from it. Now give me a renovation design, a complete plan for doing it, and the ability to put it out for bid." Who will create these capabilities? Powerful tech companies? Brands that already have relationships in their relevant categories? New, focused disruptors? The game is just starting, but the needed capabilities and business philosophies are already taking shape.

A Broader Journey with Broader Boundaries

In a world where generative AI and all the other evolving AI systems proliferate, building an offering requires focusing on the broadest possible view of your pool of data, of the journeys you can enable, and the risks they raise.

Bring data together

Solving for a customer's complete needs will require pulling from information across your company and likely beyond your boundaries. One of the biggest challenges for most applications—and actually, for most IT departments—is bringing together data from disparate systems. Many AI systems can write the code needed to understand the schemas of two different databases and integrate them into one repository, which can save several steps in standardizing data schemas. AI teams still need to dedicate time for data cleansing and data governance (arguably even more so); for example, aligning on the right definitions of key data features. However, with AI capabilities in hand, the next steps in the process to bring the data together become easier.

Narrative AI, for example, offers a marketplace for buying and selling data, along with data collaboration software that allows companies to import data from anywhere into their own repositories, aligned to their schema, with merely a click. Data from across a company—or from partners or from sellers of data—can be integrated and then used for modeling in a flash.

Combining proprietary data with public data, data from other available AI tools, and data from many external parties can serve to dramatically improve the AI's ability to understand one's context, predict what is being asked, and have a broader pool from which to execute a command.

The old rule around "garbage in, garbage out" still applies, however. Especially when it comes to integrating third-party data, it is important to cross-check the accuracy with internal data before integrating it into the underlying dataset; for example, one fashion brand recently found that gender data purchased from a third-party source didn't match its internal data 50% of the time. Source and reliability matter.

The "rules layer" becomes even more critical

Without obvious restrictions on what a customer can ask for in an input box, the AI needs to have guidelines to ensure that it responds appropriately to things beyond its means or that are inappropriate. This amplifies the need for a sharp focus on the *rules layer*, where the experienced designers, marketers, and business decision-makers set the target parameters for the AI to optimize.

For example, for an airline brand that leveraged AI to decide on the "next best conversation" to engage in with customers, we set rules around what products could be marketed to which customers, what copy could be used in which jurisdictions, and rules around antirepetition to ensure customers didn't get bombarded with irrelevant messages.

These constraints become even more critical in the era of generative AI. As pioneers of these solutions are finding, customers will be quick to point out when the machine "breaks" and produces nonsensical solutions. The best approaches will therefore start small and be tailored to specific solutions where the rules can be tightly defined and human decision-makers will be able to design rules for edge cases.

Deliver the end-to-end journey, and the specific use cases involved

Customers will just ask for what they need and will seek the simplest and/or most cost-effective way to get it done. What is the true end goal of the customer? How far can you get in satisfying it? With the ability to move information more easily across parties, you can build partnerships for data and for execution of the actions to help a customer through their journey; therefore, your ecosystem of business relationships will differentiate your brand.

In his impressive demo of how HubSpot is incorporating generative AI into ChatSpot, Dharmesh Shah,
HubSpot's CTO and founder, lays out how they are
mingling the capabilities of HubSpot with OpenAI, and
with other tools.[2] Not only does he show HubSpot's interface reduced to just a single text entry prompt, but
he also shows new capabilities that extend well beyond
HubSpot's current borders. A salesperson seeking to send
an email to a business leader at a target company can use
ChatSpot to perform research on the company, on the
target business leader, and then draft an email that in-
corporates both information from the research and from
what it knows about the salesperson themselves. The resulting email draft can then be edited, sent, and tracked
by HubSpot's system, and the target business leader automatically entered into a contact database with all associ-
ated information.

The power of connected information, automatic code
creation, and generated output is leading many other
companies to extend their borders, not as conventional
vertical or horizontal expansion, but as *journey expansion*. When you can offer services based on a simple
user command, those commands will reflect the customer's true goal and the total solution they seek, not
just a small component that you may have been dealing
with before.

Differentiate via your ecosystem

Solving for those broader needs inevitably will pull you into new kinds of partner relationships. As you build out your end-to-end journey capabilities, how you construct those business relationships will be critical new bases for strategy. How trustworthy, how well permissioned, how timely, how comprehensive, how biased is their data? How will they use data your brand sends out? What is the basis of your relationship, quality control, and data integration? Prenegotiated privileged partnerships? A simple vendor relationship? How are you charging for the broader service, and how will the parties involved get their cut?

Similar to how search brands like Google, e-commerce marketplaces like Amazon, and recommendation engines like Tripadvisor become gateways for sellers, more brands can become front-end navigators for a customer journey if they can offer quality partners, experience personalization, and simplicity. CVS could become a full health network coordinator that health providers, health tech, wellness services, pharma, and other support services will plug into. When its app can let you simply ask: "How can you help me lose 30 pounds?" or "How can you help me deal with my increasing arthritis?" the end-to-end program it can generate and then completely manage, through prompts to you and information passed around its network, will be a critical differentiator in how CVS, as a brand, builds loyalty, captures your data, and uses that to keep increasing service quality.

Prioritize safety, fairness, privacy, security, and transparency

The way you manage data becomes part of your brand, and the outcomes for your customers will have edge cases and bias risks that you should seek out and mitigate. We are all reading stories of how people are pushing generative AI systems, such as ChatGPT, to extremes and getting back what the application's developers call "hallucinations," or bizarre responses. We are also seeing responses that come back as solid assertions of wrong facts. Or responses that are derived from biased bases of data that can lead to dangerous outcomes for some populations. Companies are also getting "outed" for sharing private customer information with other parties without the customers' permission— clearly not for the benefit of their customers per se.

The risks—from the core data, to the management of data, to the nature of the output of the generative AI— will keep multiplying. Some companies have created new positions for chief customer protection officers whose role is to stay ahead of potential risk scenarios and, more importantly, to build safeguards into how product managers are developing and managing the systems. Risk committees on corporate boards are already bringing in new experts and expanding their purviews, but more action has to happen preemptively. Testing data pools for bias; understanding where data came from and its copyright, accuracy, and privacy risks; managing explicit customer permissions; limiting where information can go; and constantly testing the application for edge cases where customers could push it to extremes are all critical processes companies should build into their core product management discipline and add onto the questions that top management routinely has to ask. Boards will expect to see dashboards on these kinds of activities, and other external watchdogs, including lawyers representing legal challenges, will demand them as well.

Is it worth it? The risks will constantly multiply, and the costs of creating structures to manage those risks will be real. We've only begun to figure out how to manage bias, accuracy, copyright, privacy, and manipulated ranking risks at scale. The opacity of the systems often makes it impossible to explain how an outcome happened if some kind of audit is necessary.

Nonetheless, the capabilities of generative AI are not only available—they are the fastest-growing class of applications ever. Their accuracy will improve as the pool of tapped data increases and as parallel AI systems as well as "humans in the loop" work to find and remedy those nasty hallucinations.

The potential for simplicity, personalization, and democratization of access to new and existing applications will not only pull in hundreds of startups but also tempt many established brands into creating new AI-forward offerings. If brands can do more than just amuse a customer and actually take them through more of the requirements of their journey than ever before—and do so in a way that inspires trust—they could open up new sources of revenue from the services they can enable beyond their currently narrow borders. For the right use cases, speed and personalization could possibly be worth a price premium. But more likely, the automation abilities of AI will pull costs out of the overall system and put pressure on all participants to manage efficiently and compete accordingly.

We are now opening up a real new dialogue between brands and their customers. Literal conversations—not like the esoteric descriptions of what happened in the earlier days of digital interaction. Now we are talking back and forth. Getting things done. Together. Simply. In a trustworthy fashion. Just how the customer wants it. The race is on to see which brands can deliver.

TAKEAWAYS

Generative AI will change the way businesses develop customer-focused products, leading to new levels of personalization and customization.

✓ Generative AI can "generate" text, speech, images, music, video, and code.

✓ When that capability is joined with a feed of a customer's own information, the ease by which brands can assist customers along their journeys increases dramatically.

✓ Corporations using AI should collect and combine data from several sources, but they must be aware that not all of them may be reliable.

✓ Rules must be developed to guarantee that the AI responds appropriately. Data bias risks need to be reduced and managed.

NOTES

1. David C. Edelman and Mark Abraham, "Customer Experience in the Age of AI," *Harvard Business Review*, March–April 2022, https://hbr.org/2022/03/customer-experience-in-the-age-of-ai.

2. Dharmesh Shah, "Say Hi to ChatSpot.ai: The All-in-One A.I. Powered Chat App for Growing Better," YouTube video, March 6, 2023, https://www.youtube.com/watch?v=fayBEXSKyoI&t=5s.

Adapted from content posted on hbr.org, April 12, 2023 (product #H07KSV).

2

HOW NETWORK EFFECTS MAKE AI SMARTER

by Sheen S. Levine and Dinkar Jain

I n 2022, when OpenAI introduced ChatGPT, industry observers responded with both praise and worry. We heard how the technology can abolish computer programmers, teachers, financial traders and analysts, graphic designers, and artists. Fearing that AI would kill the college essay, universities rushed to revise curricula. Perhaps the most immediate impact, some said, was that ChatGPT could reinvent or even replace the traditional internet search engine. Search and the related ads bring in the vast majority of Google's revenue. Will chatbots kill Google?

ChatGPT is a remarkable demonstration of machine learning technology, but it is barely viable as a stand-alone service. To appropriate its technological prowess, OpenAI needed a partner. So we weren't surprised when the company quickly announced a deal with Microsoft. The union of the AI startup and the legacy tech company may finally pose a credible threat to Google's dominance, upping the stakes in the AI arms race. It also offers a lesson in the forces that will dictate which companies will thrive and which will falter in deploying this technology.

To understand what compelled OpenAI to ally itself with Bing (and why Google may still triumph), we consider how this technology differs from past developments such as the telephone or market platforms like Uber or Airbnb. In each of those examples, network effects—where the value of a product goes up as it gains users—played a major role in shaping how those products grew and which companies succeeded. Generative AI services like ChatGPT are subject to similar, but distinct, kinds of network effects. To choose strategies that work with AI, managers and entrepreneurs must grasp how these new kinds of AI network effects work.

Network Effects Work Differently for AI

AI's value lies in accurate predictions and suggestions. But unlike traditional products and services, which rely on turning supplies (like electricity or human capital) into outputs (like light or tax advice), AI requires large datasets that must be kept fresh through back-and-forth customer interactions. To remain competitive, an AI operator must corral data, analyze it, offer predictions, and then seek feedback to sharpen subsequent suggestions. The value of the system depends on—and increases with—data that arrives from users.

The technology's performance—its ability to accurately predict and suggest—hinges on an economic principle called *data network effects* (some prefer *data-driven learning*). These are distinct from the familiar direct network effects, like those that make a telephone more valuable as subscribers grow (because there are more people you can call). They are also different from indirect or second-order network effects, which describe how a growing number of buyers invites more sellers to a platform and vice versa—shopping on Etsy or booking on Airbnb becomes more attractive when more sellers are present.

Data network effects are a new form: Like the more familiar effects, the more users, the more valuable the technology is. But here, the value comes not from the number of peers (as with the telephone) or the presence of many buyers and sellers (as on platforms like Etsy). Rather, the effects stem from the nature of the technology: AI improves through reinforcement learning—predictions followed by feedback. As its intelligence increases, the system makes better predictions, enhancing its usefulness, attracting new users and retaining existing ones. More users mean more responses, which further prediction accuracy, creating a virtuous cycle.

Take, for example, Google Maps. It uses AI to recommend the fastest route to your destination. This ability hinges on anticipating the traffic patterns in alternative paths, which it does by drawing on data that arrives from many users. The more people use the app, the more historical and concurrent data it accumulates. With piles of data, Google can compare myriad predictions to actual outcomes: *Did you arrive at the time predicted by the app?* To perfect the predictions, the app also needs your impressions: *How good were the instructions?* As objective facts and subjective reviews accumulate, network effects kick in. These effects improve predictions and elevate the app's value for users—and for Google.

Once we understand how network effects drive AI, we can imagine the new strategies the technology requires.

OpenAI and Microsoft

Let's start with the marriage of OpenAI and Microsoft. When we beta-tested ChatGPT, we were impressed with its creative, humanlike responses, but recognized it was stuck. It relied on a bunch of data last collected in 2021, but was missing information such as recent events and the current weather. Even worse, it lacked a robust feedback loop: You couldn't ring the alarm bell when suggestions were hallucinatory (the company did allow a "thumbs down" response). Yet by linking to Microsoft, OpenAI found a way to test the predictions. What Bing users ask—and how they rate the answers—is crucial to updating and improving ChatGPT. The next step, we imagine, is Microsoft feeding the algorithm with the vast cloud of user data it maintains. As it digests untold numbers of Excel sheets, PowerPoint presentations, Word documents, and LinkedIn résumés, ChatGPT will get better at recreating them, to the joy (or horror) of office dwellers.

There are at least three broad lessons here.

- First, *feedback is crucial.* To remain intelligent, an algorithm needs a data stream of current user choices and rating of past suggestions. Without feedback, even the best algorithm won't remain smart for long. As OpenAI realized, even the most sophisticated models need to be linked to ever-flowing data sources. AI entrepreneurs should remember this.

- Second, executives should *routinize meticulous gathering of information* to maximize the benefits of these effects. They ought to traverse the typical financial and operational records. Useful bits of data can be found everywhere—inside and outside the corporation. Data may come from interactions with buyers, suppliers, and coworkers. A retailer, for example, could track what consumers looked at, what they placed in their cart, and what they ultimately paid for. Cumulatively, these minute details can vastly improve the predictions of an AI system. Even infrequent data bits, including those outside the company's control, might be worth collecting. Weather data helps Google Maps predict traffic. Tracking the keywords recruiters use to search résumés can help LinkedIn offer winning tips for job seekers.

- Finally, *everyone should consider the data they share, intentionally or not.* Facts and feedback are essential for building better predictions. But the value of your data can be captured by someone else. Executives should consider whose AI stands to benefit from the data they share (or allow access to). Sometimes, they should limit sharing. For instance, when Uber drivers navigate with the Waze app, they help Google, the app's owner, to estimate the frequency and length of ride-hailing trips. As Google considers operating autonomous taxis, such data could be invaluable. When a brand like Adidas sells on Amazon, it allows the retail behemoth to estimate demand across brands (comparing with Nike) and categories (shoes) plus the price sensitivity of buyers. The results could be fed to a competitor—or benefit Amazon's private label offerings. To counter that, executives can sidestep platform intermediaries or third parties. They can negotiate data access. They can strive to maintain direct contact with customers. Sometimes, the best solution may be for data owners to band and share in a data exchange, like banks did when establishing ways to share data on creditworthiness.

When you consider AI network effects, you can better understand the technology's future. You can also see how these effects, like other network effects, tend to make the rich even richer. The dynamics behind AI mean that early movers may be rewarded handsomely and followers, however quick, may be left on the sidelines. It also implies that when one has access to an AI algorithm and a flow of data, advantages accumulate over time and can't be easily surmounted. For executives, entrepreneurs, policy makers, and everyone else, the best (and worst) about AI is yet to come.

Data network effects have allowed AI to become smarter and more powerful, refining and improving its accuracy over time. AI can gain from an accumulation of data collected through each user's experience by utilizing the power of customer interactions, predictions, and feedback.

- ✓ Feedback is crucial for generative AI algorithms to perform. Without constant streams of customer interactions, even the best algorithm won't remain smart for long.

- ✓ Companies should routinize meticulous gathering of information to maximize the benefits of data network effects.

✓ Everyone should consider the data they share. Facts and feedback are essential for building better predictions, but the value of your data can be captured by someone else.

Adapted from content posted on hbr.org, March 14, 2023 (product #H07JCQ).

3

A FRAMEWORK FOR PICKING THE RIGHT GENERATIVE AI PROJECT

by Marc Zao-Sanders and Marc Ramos

There has been a huge amount of hype and speculation about the implications of large language models (LLMs) such as OpenAI's ChatGPT, Google's Bard, Anthropic's Claude, Meta's LLaMA, and GPT-4. ChatGPT, in particular, reached 100 million users in two months, making it the fastest-growing consumer application of all time.

It isn't clear yet just what kind of impact LLMs will have, and opinions vary hugely. Many experts argue that LLMs will have little impact at all (early academic research suggests that the capability of LLMs is restricted to formal linguistic competence) or that even a near-infinite volume of text-based training data is still severely limiting. Others, such as Wharton professor Ethan Mollick, argue the opposite: "The businesses that understand the significance of this change—and act on it first—will be at a considerable advantage."[1]

What we do know now is that generative AI has captured the imagination of the wider public and that it is able to produce first drafts and generate ideas virtually instantaneously. We also know that it can struggle with accuracy.

Despite the open questions about this new technology, companies are searching for ways to apply it—now. Is there a way to cut through the polarizing arguments, hype, and hyperbole and think clearly about where the technology will hit home first? We believe there is.

Risk and Demand

On risk, how likely and how damaging is the possibility of untruths and inaccuracies being generated and disseminated? On demand, what is the real and sustainable need for this kind of output, beyond the current buzz?

It's useful to consider these variables together. Thinking of them in a 2×2 matrix provides a more nuanced, one-size-doesn't-fit-all analysis of what may be coming. Indeed, risks and demands differ across different industries and business activities. We have placed some common cross-industry use cases in figure 3-1.

Think about where your business function or industry might sit. For your use case, how much is the risk reduced by introducing a step for human validation? How much might that slow down the process and reduce the demand?

The top-left box—where the consequence of errors is relatively low and market demand is high—will inevitably develop faster and further. For these use cases, there is a ready-made incentive for companies to find solutions, and there are fewer hurdles for their success. We should expect to see a combination of raw, immediate utilization of the technology as well as third-party tools that leverage generative AI and its APIs for their particular domain.

This is happening already in marketing, where several startups have found innovative ways to apply LLMs to generate content marketing copy and ideas and have achieved unicorn status. Marketing requires a lot of idea generation and iteration, messaging tailored to specific audiences, and the production of text-rich messages that

FIGURE 3-1

Picking a generative AI project

As your company decides where to start exploring generative AI, it's important to balance risk and demand. One way to think about that is to ask two questions: "How damaging would it be if untruths and inaccuracies were generated and disseminated?" (risk) and "What is the real and sustainable need for this kind of output, beyond the current buzz?" (demand). Consider using this matrix—populated with common, cross-industry use cases—to identify the most valuable, least-risky applications for your company.

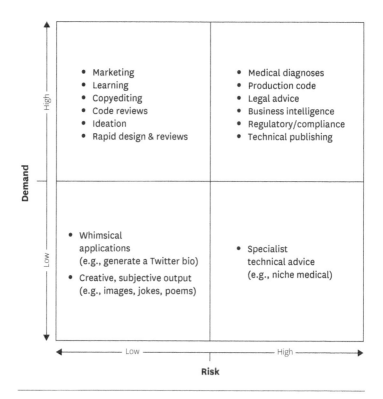

can engage and influence audiences. In other words, there are clear uses and demonstrated demand. Importantly, there's also a wealth of examples that can be used to guide an AI to match style and content. On the other hand, most marketing copy isn't fact-heavy, and the facts that are important can be corrected in editing.

Looking at the matrix, you can find that there are other opportunities that have received less attention, for instance, learning. Like marketing, creating content for learning—for our purposes, let's use the example of internal corporate learning tools—requires engaging and effective text and a clear understanding of its audience's interests. There's also likely content that can be used to guide a generative AI tool. Priming it with existing documentation, you can ask it to rewrite, synthesize, and update the materials you have to better speak to different audiences or to make learning material more adaptable to different contexts.

Generative AI's capabilities could also allow learning materials to be delivered differently—woven into the flow of everyday work or replacing clunky FAQs, bulging knowledge centers, and ticketing systems.

The other uses in the high-demand/low-risk box above follow similar logic: They're for tasks where people are often involved, and the risk of AI playing fast and loose with facts are low. Take the examples of asking the AI to review text: You can feed it a draft, give it some instructions (you want a more detailed version, a softer tone, a five-point summary, or suggestions of how to make the text more concise), and review its suggestions. As a second pair of eyes, the technology is ready to use right now. If you want ideas to feed a brainstorm—steps to take when hiring a modern multimedia designer or what to buy a 4-year-old who likes trains for her birthday—generative AI will be a quick, reliable, and safe bet, as those ideas are likely not in the final product.

Filling in the matrix with tasks that are part of your company's or team's work can help draw similar parallels. Assessing risk and demand and considering the shared elements of particular tasks can give you a useful starting point and help you draw connections and see opportunities. It can also help you see where it doesn't make sense to invest time and resources.

The other three quadrants aren't places where you should rush to find uses for generative AI tools. When demand is low, there's little motivation for people to utilize or develop the technology. Producing haikus in the style of a Shakespearian pirate may make us laugh and drop our jaws today, but such party tricks will not keep our attention for very much longer. And in cases where there is demand but high risk, general trepidation and regulation will slow the pace of progress. Considering your own 2×2 matrix, you can put the uses listed there aside for the time being.

Low Risk Is Still Risk

A mild cautionary note: Even in corporate learning where, as we have argued, the risk is low, there is risk. Generative AI is vulnerable to bias and errors, just as humans are. If you assume the outputs of a generative AI system are good to go and immediately distribute them to your entire workforce, there is plenty of risk. Your ability to strike the right balance between speed and quality will be tested.

So take the initial output as a first iteration. Improve on it with a more detailed prompt or two. And then tweak that output yourself, adding the real-world knowledge, nuance, even artistry and humor that, for a little while longer, only a human has.

TAKEAWAYS

Generative AI is able to produce first drafts and generate ideas virtually instantaneously, but it can also struggle with accuracy and ethical problems. How should companies navigate the risks in their pursuit of its rewards?

✓ In picking use cases, companies need to balance risk (How likely and how damaging is the possibility of untruths and inaccuracies being generated and disseminated?) and demand (What is the real and sustainable need for this kind of output, beyond the current buzz?).

✓ A 2×2 matrix that plots risk and demand can help companies choose the best generative AI projects and improve their chances of success.

✓ Companies should run experiments that fit into the high-demand/low-risk box of the matrix. The other three quadrants aren't places where companies should rush to find uses for generative AI tools.

NOTE

1. Ethan Mollick, "ChatGPT Is a Tipping Point for AI," hbr.org, December 14, 2022, https://hbr.org/2022/12/chatgpt-is-a-tipping-point-for-ai.

Adapted from content posted on hbr.org, March 29, 2023 (product #H07J5S).

HOW GENERATIVE AI COULD DISRUPT CREATIVE WORK

by David De Cremer, Nicola Morini Bianzino, and Ben Falk

The "creator economy" is currently valued at around $14 billion per year. Enabled by new digital channels, independent writers, podcasters, artists, and musicians can connect with audiences directly to make their own incomes. Internet platforms such as Substack, Flipboard, and Steemit enable individuals not only to create content but also to become independent producers and brand managers of their work. While many kinds of work were being disrupted by new technologies, these platforms offered people new ways to make a living through human creativity.

In the face of technological change, creativity is often held up as a uniquely human quality, less vulnerable to the forces of technological disruption and critical for the future. Indeed, behavioral researchers even call the skill of creativity a human masterpiece.

Today, however, generative AI applications such as ChatGPT and Midjourney are threatening to upend this special status and significantly alter creative work, both independent and salaried. Jobs focused on delivering content—writing, creating images, coding, and other jobs that typically require an intensity of knowledge and information—now seem likely to be uniquely affected by generative AI.

What isn't clear yet is what shape this kind of impact will take. We propose three possible—but, importantly, not mutually exclusive—scenarios for how this development might unfold. In doing so, we highlight risks and opportunities and conclude by offering recommendations for what companies should do today to prepare for this brave new world.

Three Possible Futures

An explosion of AI-assisted innovation

Today, most businesses recognize the importance of adopting AI to promote the efficiency and performance of their human workforce. For example, AI is being used to augment health-care professionals' job performance in high-stakes work, advising physicians during surgery and used as a tool in cancer screenings. It's also being used in customer service, a lower-stakes context. And robotics is used to make warehouses run with greater speed and reliability, as well as reducing costs.

With the arrival of generative AI, we're seeing experiments with augmentation in more creative work. Just back in 2021, GitHub introduced GitHub Copilot, an AI "pair programmer" that aids human coders.[1] More recently, designers, filmmakers, and advertising execs have started using image generators such as DALL-E 2. These tools don't require users to be very tech savvy. In fact, most of these applications are so easy to use that even children with elementary-level verbal skills can use them to create content right now. Pretty much everyone can make use of them.

This scenario isn't (necessarily) a threat to people who do creative work. Rather than putting many creators out of work, AI will support humans to do the work they already perform, simply allowing them to do it with greater speed and efficiency. In this scenario, productivity would rise as reliance on generative AI tools that use natural language reduces the time and effort required to come up with new ideas or pieces of text. Of course, humans will still have to devote time to possibly correct and edit the newly generated information, but overall, creative projects should be able to move forward more quickly (see chapter 5, "How Generative AI Can Augment Human Creativity").

We can already glimpse what such future holds: With reduced barriers to entry, we can expect many more people to engage in creative work. GitHub Copilot doesn't replace the human coder, but it does make coding easier for novices, as they can rely on the knowledge and vast reams of data embedded within the model rather than having to learn everything from scratch. If more people learn "prompt engineering"—the skill of asking the machine the right questions—AI will be able to produce very relevant and meaningful content that humans will need to edit only somewhat before they can put it to use. This higher level of efficiency can be facilitated by having people speak instructions to a computer via advanced voice-to-text algorithms, which will then be interpreted and executed by an AI like ChatGPT.

The ability to quickly and easily retrieve, contextualize, and interpret knowledge may be the most powerful business application of large language models. A natural language interface combined with a powerful AI algorithm will help humans in coming up more quickly with a larger number of ideas and solutions that they subsequently can experiment with to reveal more and better creative output. Overall, this scenario paints a world of faster innovation where machine-augmented human creativity will enable mainly rapid iteration.

Machines monopolize creativity

A second possible scenario is that unfair algorithmic competition and inadequate governance leads to the crowding out of authentic human creativity. Here, human writers, producers, and creators are drowned out by a tsunami of algorithmically generated content, with some talented creators even opting out of the market. If that were to happen, then an important question that we need to address is: How will we generate new ideas?

A nascent version of this scenario might already exist. For example, recent lawsuits against prominent generative AI platforms allege copyright infringement on a massive scale. What makes this issue even more fraught is that intellectual property laws have not caught up with the technological progress made in the field of AI research. It's quite possible that governments will spend decades fighting over how to balance incentives for technical innovation while retaining incentives for authentic human creation—a route that would be a terrific loss for human creativity.

In this scenario, generative AI significantly changes the incentive structure for creators and raises risks for businesses and society. If cheaply made generative AI undercuts authentic human content, there's a real risk that innovation will slow down over time as humans make less and less new art and content. Creators are already in intense competition for human attention spans, and this kind of competition—and pressure—will only rise further if there is unlimited content on demand. Extreme content abundance, far beyond what we've seen with any digital disruption to date, will inundate us with noise, and we'll need to find new techniques and strategies to manage the deluge.

This scenario could also mean fundamental changes to what content creation looks like. If production costs fall close to nothing, that opens up the possibility of reaching specific—and often less included—audiences through extreme personalization and versioning. In fact, we expect the pressure to personalize to go up fast because generative AI carries such great potential to create content that is increasingly representative of the specific consumer. As a case in point, BuzzFeed announced it will personalize its content such as quizzes and tailor-made rom-com pitches with OpenAI's tools.[2]

If the practice of enhanced personalized experiences is applied broadly, then we run the risk of losing the shared experience of watching the same film, reading the same book, and consuming the same news. In that case, it will be easier to create politically divisive viral content and significant volumes of mis/disinformation as the average quality of content declines alongside the share of authentic human content. Both would likely worsen filter bubble effects, where algorithmic bias skews or limits what an individual sees online.

Yet even in this relative dystopia, there remains a significant role for humans to make recommendations of existing content in this ecosystem. As in other very large content markets, like music streaming services, curation will become more valuable relative to creation as search costs rise. At the same time, however, high search costs will lock in existing artists at the expense of new ones, concentrating and bifurcating the market. This will result in a small handful of established artists dominating the market with a long tail of creators retaining minimal market share.

"Human-made" commands a premium

The third potential scenario that we could see develop is one where the "techlash" against giant tech companies regains speed, this time with a focus against algorithmically generated content. One plausible effect of being inundated with synthetic creative outputs is that people will begin to value authentic creativity over generated content and may be willing to pay a premium for it. While generative models demonstrate remarkable and sometimes emergent capabilities, they suffer from problems with accuracy, frequently producing text that sounds legitimate but is riddled with factual errors and erroneous logic. For obvious reasons, humans might demand greater accuracy from their content providers and may therefore rely more on trusted human sources than on machine-generated information.

In this scenario, humans maintain a competitive advantage against algorithmic competition. The uniqueness of human creativity, including awareness of social and cultural context both across borders and through time, will become important leverage. Culture changes much more quickly than generative algorithms can be trained, so humans maintain a dynamism that algorithms cannot compete against. In fact, it is likely that humans will retain the ability to make significant leaps of creativity, even if algorithmic capabilities improve incrementally.

In the development of this scenario, it follows that political leadership will have to strengthen governance to deal with the potential downside risks. For instance, content moderation needs are likely to explode as information platforms are overwhelmed with false or misleading content, and therefore must be countered with human intervention and carefully designed governance frameworks.

How to Prepare for Generative AI

Creativity has always been a critical prerequisite for any company's innovation process and hence competitiveness. Not too long ago, the business of creativity was a uniquely human endeavor. However, as we've illustrated, the arrival of generative AI is about to change all this. To be prepared, we need to understand the accompanying threats and challenges. Once we understand what is to change and how, we can prepare for a future where the creativity business will be a function of human–machine

collaborations. Below, we provide three recommendations that workers should consider as they adopt generative AI to create business value and profit in today's
creative industries.

Prepare for disruption, and not only to your job

Generative AI could be the biggest change in the cost
structure of information production since the creation
of the printing press in 1439. The centuries that followed
featured rapid innovation, sociopolitical volatility, and
economic disruption across a swath of industries as the
cost of acquiring knowledge and information fell precipi-
tously. We are in the very early stages of the generative
AI revolution. We expect the near future therefore to be
more volatile than the recent past.

Invest in your ontology

Codifying, digitizing, and structuring the knowledge
you create will be a critical value driver in the decades to
come. Generative AI and large language models enable
knowledge and skills to transmit more easily across teams
and business units, accelerating learning and innovation.

Get comfortable talking to AI

As AI becomes a partner in intellectual endeavors, it will increasingly augment the effectiveness and creativity of our human intelligence. Knowledge workers therefore will need to learn how to best prompt the machine to perform their work. Get started today, experimenting with generative AI tools to develop skills in prompt engineering, a prerequisite skill for creative workers in the decade to come.

. . .

With generative AI, a major disruptor of our creative work has emerged. Businesses and the world at large will be impatient to apply the new emerging technologies to boost our level of productivity and content generation. Be prepared to invest significant time and effort to master the art of creativity in a world dominated by generative AI.

At the same time, we also need to seriously consider what these new technologies mean for being a creative human today and how much importance we wish to assign to the role of human authenticity in art and content. In other words, with generative AI at the forefront of our work existence, what will our relationship with creativity be? It was Einstein who said that creativity is intelligence having fun. Creative work is thus also something that brings meaning and emotion to the lives of humans.

From that perspective, businesses and society will be responsible to decide how much of the creative work will ultimately be done by AI and how much by humans. Finding the balance here will be an important challenge when we move ahead with integrating generative AI in our daily work existence.

Through the automation and customization of content creation, generative AI has the potential to transform the creative process. Applications that use generative AI, including ChatGPT and Midjourney, are proliferating and pose a threat to all types of creative work.

✓ There are three scenarios that could occur because of generative AI's impact on creativity: an explosion of AI-assisted innovation, the monopolization of creativity by machines, or a premium placed on human-produced content.

✓ Individuals and businesses should be ready for disruption, invest in knowledge ontologies, and become comfortable speaking with AI.

✓ When incorporating generative AI into creative work, we must consider what we want our continuing relationship with human creativity to be.

NOTES

1. Nat Friedman, "Introducing GitHub Copilot: Your AI Pair Programmer," GitHub blog, June 29, 2021, https://github.blog/2021-06 -29-introducing-github-copilot-ai-pair-programmer/.

2. James Vincent, "BuzzFeed Says It Will Use AI Tools from OpenAI to Personalize Its Content," The Verge, January 21, 2023, https://www.theverge.com/2023/1/26/23572834/buzzfeed-using-ai -tools-personalize-generate-content-openai.

Adapted from content posted on hbr.org, April 13, 2023 (product #H07LIA).

5

HOW GENERATIVE AI CAN AUGMENT HUMAN CREATIVITY

by Tojin T. Eapen, Daniel J. Finkenstadt, Josh Folk, and Lokesh Venkataswamy

There is tremendous apprehension about the potential of generative AI to replace people in many jobs. But one of the biggest opportunities generative AI offers to businesses and governments is to augment human creativity and overcome the challenges of democratizing innovation.

The term *democratizing innovation* was coined by MIT's Eric von Hippel, who, since the mid-1970s, has been researching and writing about the potential for users of products and services to develop what they need themselves rather than simply relying on companies to do so. In the past two decades or so, the notion of deeply involving users in the innovation process has taken off, and today companies use crowdsourcing and innovation contests to generate a multitude of new ideas. However, many enterprises struggle to capitalize on these contributions because of four challenges.

First, efforts to democratize innovation may result in evaluation overload. Crowdsourcing, for instance, may produce a flood of ideas, many of which end up being dumped or disregarded because companies have no efficient way to evaluate them or merge incomplete or minor ideas that could prove potent in combination.

Second, companies may fall prey to the curse of expertise. Domain experts who are best at generating and identifying *feasible* ideas often struggle with generating or even accepting *novel* ideas.

Third, people who lack domain expertise may identify novel ideas but may be unable to provide the details that would make the ideas feasible. They can't translate messy ideas into coherent designs.

And finally, companies have trouble seeing the forest for the trees. Organizations focus on synthesizing a host of customer requirements but struggle to produce a comprehensive solution that will appeal to the community at large.

Our research and our experience working with companies, academic institutions, governments, and militaries on hundreds of innovation efforts—some with and some without the use of generative AI—have demonstrated that this technology can help organizations overcome these challenges. It can augment the creativity of employees and customers and help them generate and identify novel ideas—and improve the quality of raw ideas. We have observed the following five ways.

Promote Divergent Thinking

Generative AI can support divergent thinking by making associations among remote concepts and producing ideas drawn from them. Here's an example of how we used Midjourney, a text-to-image algorithm that can detect analogical resemblances between images, to generate novel product designs based on textual prompts from a human. (We used Midjourney, ChatGPT, and Stable Diffusion for the examples in this article, but they are just a few of a host of generative AI tools that are now available.) We asked Midjourney to create an image that combined an elephant and a butterfly, and it produced the chimera we dubbed "phantafly."

We then used the detailed rendering from Midjourney to inspire prompts in Stable Diffusion, another popular text-to-image model. Stable Diffusion generated a range of ideas for different product categories, including chairs and artisanal chocolate candies (see figures 5-1 and 5-2).

Rapidly and inexpensively producing a plethora of designs in this way allows a company to evaluate a wide

FIGURE 5-1

Phantafly-inspired chair concepts by Stable Diffusion

FIGURE 5-2

Phantafly-inspired artisanal chocolate concepts by Stable Diffusion

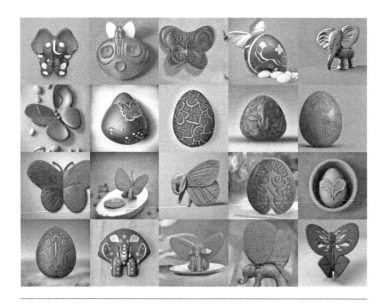

range of product concepts quickly. For example, a clothing company that uses generative AI to create new designs for T-shirts could stay on top of trends and offer a constantly changing selection of products to customers.

Consider another example of how this technology can connect ideas to create concepts that an individual or a team might never have come up with themselves. We used ChatGPT, a type of generative AI known as a large language model, to guide the production of ideas. We asked it to generate ideas through a process of *trisociation*—connecting three distinct entities (an extension of the bisociation creativity technique). Our team gave ChatGPT the following prompt: "You will play the role of an ideator. You will randomly generate 10 common nouns. You will then randomly select any two of the 10 nouns. You will then ask me for a third noun. You will generate a business idea by combining or associating the two nouns you identified and the noun I identified."

ChatGPT generated the nouns *food* and *technology*. When prompted, we provided the additional noun *car*. ChatGPT produced the following business idea in short order: "A smart food-delivery service that uses self-driving cars to transport meals to customers. The technology aspect could involve using AI to optimize delivery routes, track food temperature in real time, and provide customers with real-time updates on the status of their orders. The service could target busy professionals and families who want convenient and healthy meal options without sacrificing taste and quality."

In a separate round, ChatGPT produced the nouns *airline* and *chair*. When prompted, we provided *university*, and ChatGPT came up with a business concept that provides a convenient, cost-effective way for students and academics to travel to conferences and workshops around the world along with access to a library of educational books during the flight. It proposed that the company be called Fly and Study or Edu-Fly.

Challenge Expertise Bias

During the early stages of new-product development, atypical designs created by generative AI can inspire designers to think beyond their preconceptions of what is possible or desirable in a product in terms of both form and function. This approach can lead to solutions that humans might never have imagined using a traditional approach, where the functions are determined first and the form is then designed to accommodate them. These inputs can help overcome biases such as design fixation (an overreliance on standard design forms), functional fixedness (a lack of ability to imagine a use beyond the traditional one), and the Einstellung effect, where individuals' previous experiences impede them from considering new ways to solve problems.

Here's an example of this process. We asked Stable Diffusion to generate generic designs of crab-inspired toys but provided it with no functional specifications. Then we imagined functional capabilities after seeing the designs. For instance, in the collection of crab-inspired toys shown in figure 5-3, the image in the top left could be developed into a wall-climbing toy; the image next to it could be a toy that launches a small ball across a room. The crab on a plate near the center could become a slow-feeder dish for pets.

This is not a completely novel way to come up with unusual products: Much of the architecture and ride

FIGURE 5-3

Crab-inspired toy concepts by Stable Diffusion

functionality in theme parks such as Disney World has been driven by a desire to recreate scenes and characters from a story. But generative AI tools can help jump-start a company's imaginative designs.

Assist in Idea Evaluation

Generative AI tools can assist in other aspects of the front end of innovation, including by increasing the specificity of ideas and by evaluating ideas and sometimes combining them. Consider an innovation challenge where the goal is to identify ways to minimize food waste. ChatGPT assessed the pros and cons of three raw ideas: (1) packaging with dynamic expiration dates (labels that automatically change either the dates or colors based on the environmental conditions in the places where they are stored); (2) an app to help users donate food; and (3) a campaign to educate people on types of expiration dates and what they represent in terms of freshness and fitness for use. ChatGPT produced a balanced analysis of the pros and cons that mirrored what we might expect from an exchange between two interested persons discussing the merits of such ideas.

When ChatGPT evaluated the concept of dynamic expiration-date packaging, for instance, it determined that it would help consumers better understand the shelf life of products and encourage food manufacturers to produce smaller batches that would be replenished more frequently on grocery shelves. In addition, ChatGPT pointed out that dynamic expiration dates might require significant changes to the manufacturing and packaging process and as a result, could increase the costs to both manufacturers and consumers.

ChatGPT determined that the food-donation app could encourage people to use up their food before it goes bad and reduce food waste by giving unopened, edible food to those in need. It cautioned that the app could require a large user base to be effective and that the transportation and distribution of food from a wide variety of unregulated sources could pose safety concerns.

It stated that the pros of an education program for consumers were increasing consumer awareness of the meaning of different expiration labels and helping them make more-informed decisions about food purchases and waste. But ChatGPT warned that this education program could be overly complex because expiration dates are not standardized across all food products. And it cautioned that educating users on different types of expiration dates can be costly if the program is broad in scope, particularly if it involves widespread campaigns or educational materials.

Generative AI can go beyond simple pros and cons and help humans evaluate dimensions of creativity such as novelty, feasibility, specificity, impact, and workability. We asked ChatGPT to assess the same examples using these criteria.

Here is its assessment of the dynamic expiration-date packaging concept:

Novelty: Somewhat novel. There have been efforts to develop smart packaging that can extend the shelf life of food products, but the idea of dynamic expiration dates is an emerging concept.

Feasibility: May be challenging to implement as it requires the development of new packaging materials and technologies. It would also require collaboration with food manufacturers, regulators, and distributors.

Specificity: It's specific in that it addresses the problem of food waste by providing consumers with more-accurate expiration dates for their food.

Impact: Could have a significant impact on reducing food waste and improving food safety. When provided with more-accurate expiration dates, consumers would be more likely to use their food before it goes bad.

Workability: It would most likely require significant resources and expertise to develop and implement and may take several years to fully realize its potential.

Here is ChatGPT's assessment of the app for donating food close to expiration:

Novelty: Not particularly novel. There are already many programs and organizations dedicated to reducing food waste and donating surplus food to those in need.

Feasibility: Highly feasible. There are many established models and an infrastructure in place to support food donation efforts.

Specificity: Specific in its aim to reduce food waste and address issues of food insecurity.

Impact: Has the potential to make a significant impact as it addresses both food waste and hunger. By redirecting surplus food to those in need, it can help reduce food waste while also improving food security for vulnerable populations.

Workability: Highly workable in that it can be implemented quickly and at a relatively low cost. It would require partnerships with food manufacturers, distributors, and food banks, as well as volunteers to collect and distribute the donated food.

Finally, here is how ChatGPT evaluated the idea to educate users on different types of expiration dates:

Novelty: Not particularly novel. There have been efforts to educate consumers on the meaning of expiration dates and how to properly store food to extend its shelf life.

Feasibility: Highly feasible. It can be implemented through various means, such as public awareness campaigns, educational materials, and media outreach.

Specificity: Specific in its aim to educate consumers on the different expiration dates and how to properly store food to reduce food waste.

Impact: Potentially significant. Educating consumers on the different expiration dates and how to properly store food will make them more mindful of food waste and take steps to reduce it.

Workability: Highly workable and can be implemented at a relatively low cost. It would require collaboration with food industry groups, government agencies, and other organizations to develop and distribute educational materials.

Using ChatGPT's assessments, it would be relatively easy to evaluate these three concepts, or quickly score or organize them based on the criteria that matter most.

Support Idea Refinement

Generative AI tools can solve an important challenge faced in idea contests: combining or merging a large number of ideas to produce much stronger ones. For example, an organization that is trying to win a contract or a grant to develop a food-waste-reduction program can use the tools to combine the three concepts discussed earlier. We did this in two steps. First, we asked ChatGPT to flesh out each of the concepts:

- "Dynamic expiration dates are a solution aimed at reducing food waste. This involves incorporating technology into packaging that can track and adjust the shelf life of products in real time. By using sensors, the expiration date can be updated based on changes in environmental factors, providing consumers with a more accurate estimate of when a product will go bad."

- "An app that enables consumers to donate food close to its expiration date aims to reduce food waste by giving unopened, edible food to those in need. The app connects individuals who have surplus food to local organizations that can use it. By using technology to facilitate food donations, the app can help reduce food waste and provide for those in need."

- "Educating users on the different types of expiration dates can help users make informed decisions about purchasing and consuming food, reducing waste, and saving money. By clarifying the meaning of 'best before,' 'use by,' and other expiration labels, an education campaign can help users better understand how to determine if food is safe to eat and when it is time to dispose of it."

Next, we asked ChatGPT to merge all three ideas into one food-waste program. In short order it produced the following description: "The comprehensive food-waste-reduction solution involves creating smart packaging with dynamic expiration dates, establishing a program for donating surplus food, and educating the public on the importance of understanding food expiration dates. The smart packaging helps consumers make informed decisions about food freshness, the donation program ensures surplus food is put to good use, and education raises awareness about the impact of food waste. This solution has the potential to significantly reduce food waste and create a more sustainable future by empowering consumers, working with industry and government, and making better use of surplus food."

Facilitate Collaboration with and Among Users

When developing new product ideas or designs, generative AI can facilitate collaborations between a company's designers and users of a prospective product and among users themselves. In other words, the technology makes co-creation of new offerings much easier and less expensive. For example, a business can give users access to tools to generate designs and then create a personalized version of the product based on the customer's preferences. Alternatively, users' designs could be posted on a crowdsourcing platform where they are evaluated by the community. The top designs could then be further developed by additional collaborators.

To illustrate the potential, we show how a flying car—something people have been trying to develop for more than 100 years without much success—might be designed. We gave Stable Diffusion this prompt: "Design a product that can fly but also drive on the road, a flying automobile." Stable Diffusion generated several designs, and we selected what we considered to be the most promising one: the vehicle in the lower right corner of figure 5-4.

Then we asked Stable Diffusion to take that design and reimagine the concept so that the car "resembles a robot eagle." Figure 5-5 shows the variations that the

FIGURE 5-4

Stable Diffusion's concepts of a flying automobile

FIGURE 5-5

Stable Diffusion's concepts of a flying automobile that resembles a robot eagle

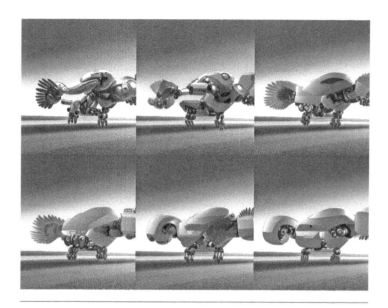

generative AI program quickly produced—from the top left design that looks most like a robot eagle to the more feasible concept of a flying automobile in the lower right corner.

A second example illustrates how designers can use such tools to collaborate on thematic variations of a structural design. They began with a flying-automobile design generated by AI and asked the tool to produce versions that resembled a dragonfly, a tiger, a tortoise, and an eagle (see figure 5-6).

An alternative approach is for human collaborators to use a tool like ChatGPT to develop details of the product and then use one like Stable Diffusion to obtain visual designs based on a series of prompts that build on one another. We gave ChatGPT a similar prompt to what we had given to Stable Diffusion: "Describe a product that can fly but also drive on the road, a flying automobile."

ChatGPT provided this description: "The flying automobile is a sleek and futuristic vehicle that is built for the ultimate adventure. It has the appearance of a stylish

FIGURE 5-6

AI-generated designs of a flying car that resemble a dragonfly, a tiger, a tortoise, and an eagle

FIGURE 5-7

Flying automobile design using Stable Diffusion to generate a design from a ChatGPT description

sports car with smooth curves and polished exterior but with hidden rotors that allow it to take flight." When we gave that description to Stable Diffusion, it provided the image shown in figure 5-7.

Next we asked ChatGPT to reimagine the description to include the information that the product must resemble a dragonfly and have illumination markers for flying at night. It came back with the following: "With its slender body, extended wings, and hidden rotors, the vehicle is reminiscent of a dragonfly come to life. The

FIGURE 5-8

Variations on the design that incorporate dragonfly details and illumination

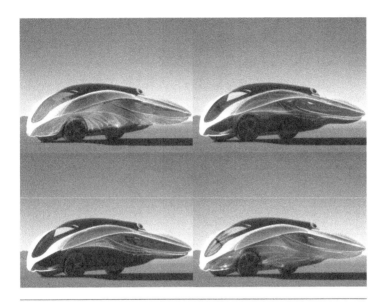

illuminated markers located along the wings and body create a stunning visual effect, helping to make the vehicle visible in the darkness." Stable Diffusion translated that description into various versions that maintained the feasible design and added elements of illumination based on the pattern of a dragonfly's wings. The images in figure 5-8 are examples.

. . .

Humans have boundless creativity. However, the challenge of communicating their concepts in written or visual form restricts vast numbers of people from contributing new ideas. Generative AI can remove this obstacle. As with any truly innovative capability, there will undoubtedly be resistance to it. Long-standing innovation processes will have to change. People with vested interests in the old way of doing things—especially those worried about being rendered obsolete—will resist. But the advantages—the opportunities to dramatically increase the number and novelty of ideas from both inside and outside the organization—will make the journey worthwhile. Generative AI's greatest potential is not replacing humans; it is to assist humans in their individual and collective efforts to create hitherto unimaginable solutions. It can truly democratize innovation.

Generative AI has the potential to augment human creativity. It enables designers to investigate concepts from several perspectives, think divergently, see beyond their own assumptions, and use data-driven insights to question those assumptions.

- ✓ AI can help solve creativity-related problems like assessment overload, expertise bias, insufficient details, and trouble understanding the bigger picture.

- ✓ Generative AI can support the examination and improvement of ideas by evaluating fresh concepts and combinations of already-existing undeveloped concepts.

- ✓ These technologies encourage user participation in the codevelopment of new products.

Adapted from an article in Harvard Business Review, *July–August 2023 (product #R2304C).*

HOW GENERATIVE AI WILL CHANGE SALES

by Prabhakant Sinha, Arun Shastri, and Sally E. Lorimer

Early in 2023, Microsoft fired a powerful salvo by launching Viva Sales, an application with embedded generative AI technology designed to help salespeople and sales managers draft tailored customer emails, get insights about customers and prospects, and generate recommendations and reminders. A few weeks later, Salesforce (the company) followed by launching Einstein GPT.

Sales, with its unstructured, highly variable, people-driven approach, has lagged behind functions such as finance, logistics, and marketing when it comes to utilizing digital technologies. But now, sales are primed to quickly become a leading adopter of generative AI. AI-powered systems are on the way to becoming every salesperson's (and every sales manager's) indispensable digital assistant.

Sales is well suited to the capabilities of generative AI models. Selling is interaction- and transaction-intensive, producing large volumes of data, including text from email chains, audio of phone conversations, and video of personal interactions. These are exactly the types of unstructured data the models are designed to work with. The creative and organic nature of selling creates immense opportunities for generative AI to interpret, learn, link, and customize.

But there are hurdles and challenges to overcome if generative AI is to realize its potential. It must be nonintrusively embedded into sales processes and operations so that sales teams can naturally integrate the capabilities into their workflow. Generative AI sometimes draws wrong, biased, or inconsistent conclusions. Although the publicly accessible models are valuable (hundreds of millions of users like us have already used ChatGPT to query the knowledge base on practically every topic), the true power for sales teams comes when models are customized and fine-tuned on company-specific data and contexts. This can be expensive and requires scarce expertise, including people with significant knowledge of AI *and* sales. So how can sales organizations harvest the value without wasting energy on heading down unproductive pathways?

What's Possible

Before addressing the *how*, consider *what* generative AI can do for sales organizations.

Reversing administrative creep

Almost every sales organization we touch is cursed with the gradual increase of administrative work over time. As selling complexity grows, so does the need for documentation, approvals, and compliance reporting. Unwittingly, the increasing use of sales technology is also a large factor. New technologies often lead to more training, more data entry, and more reports to peruse. Generative AI can reverse administrative creep; for example, by helping salespeople write emails, respond to proposal requests, organize notes, and automatically update CRM data.

Enhancing salespeople's customer interactions

The use of AI in sales has been progressing of late. We have helped many companies deploy AI-powered systems that recommend personalized content and product offers, along with the best channel for salespeople to use to connect with customers. Recommendations are based on data about the preferences and behaviors of the customer and similar customers, as well as past interactions with the customer. Salespeople accept or reject the recommendations and can rate their quality to improve the algorithms.

By layering on generative AI, the models can produce better recommendations. One example would be considering customer sentiments gleaned from the nuances of language and subtle signals of customer interest or distrust—in emails, conversations with salespeople, posts on social media sites, and more. Further, the salesperson can collaborate with the system to improve recommendations in real time. For example, after receiving a suggestion to approach a customer with a new offering, the salesperson can dig deeper—both vertically into the customer's own needs and horizontally to find other customers who might benefit from the same offering. An interactive, conversational user interface makes the application easy to use. In a truly collaborative seller–buyer environment, even the buyer can be part of the dialog.

Assisting sales managers

Sales managers spend a lot of time studying reports and analytics on sales performance. Recently, most sales reports have progressed from passive, backward-looking documents to more interactive diagnostics tools with drill-down capabilities. With generative AI, reporting systems can become even more powerful and forward-looking. Managers can pose questions to get insights for helping salespeople improve and for delivering more pointed and more motivational coaching feedback. Sales planning tasks that took weeks can be performed in an hour as managers dialogue with the system to discover opportunities, formulate key account strategies, and determine how to allocate effort to geographies, customers, products, and activities.

The Journey to Value

Generative AI is relatively new and evolving rapidly. There is a shortage of talent for defining its role, training and fine-tuning models, and developing and implementing applications. One must find pathways that guard against falsehood challenges, realize value quickly, and deliver results while keeping costs under control.

Dealing with inaccuracy and inconsistency

ChatGPT and its competitors do sometimes give inaccurate answers or draw the wrong inferences. You ask the same question twice and you get different answers. Users must know when and how to use such technologies. They must start with high but realistic expectations. There is an art to asking questions and providing successive prompts to improve the answer. Sales organizations must learn this through training, apprenticeship, and best-practice sharing.

The risk is lower when these models are fine-tuned on knowledge from the company's context. Through added data, training, and feedback, accuracy and consistency improve (just like with people!). AI-generated answers in risky contexts must be reviewed by a person. Fortunately, human review is a natural part of salespeople's and sales managers' workflow.

Realizing value quickly

As the power of this disruptive technology grows exponentially, it's possible to start realizing value in weeks, not months. One strategy for quick results is to integrate capabilities into existing sales systems. For example, generative AI can improve the tools salespeople use to write emails or develop sales presentations and proposals. It can also boost the quality of AI-generated suggestions by incorporating insights about customer sentiments. Such enhancements can happen in the background, so users benefit without needing to relearn application features. When it comes to speed of implementation, "buy" trumps "build." Although building a custom AI-powered system offers greater flexibility, doing so is time-consuming and resource-intensive. Buying an existing application reduces the need for specialized in-house talent and makes it easier to keep up with fast-changing technology.

Delivering results while controlling costs

It often makes sense to outsource capabilities while developing a small core of internal AI experts who support sales as well as other functions. The odds of success are greater when efforts to bring AI to sales are led by a "boundary spanner"—an individual who understands and is respected by technical experts as well as by sales force members. By speaking both languages, a boundary spanner can help judiciously tailor solutions so they are usable and useful for sales but also implementable and sustainable over time. Further, an agile, iterative approach to implementation keeps efforts on the path to value while encouraging continuous improvement. Key steps include rapid prototyping, testing, and iteration based on feedback from an early-experience team—a group of lead users who provide insights about system usability, value, and implementation plans.

Is AI a Productivity Aid or a Substitute for Salespeople?

We expect generative AI is to power digital assistants for nearly every salesperson and sales manager. These tools are already helping copywriters draft content and computer programmers write code, boosting their productivity by 50% or more. It can do the same for salespeople.

AI is already making customer self-service more powerful, and inside sales more potent. Consumers are increasingly using digital technology to research products and services on their own.

E-commerce has taken off in the B2B world too. Even in complex sales, digital plays an increasing role, taking on tasks such as lead generation and prioritization, product information sharing and configuring, and order placement. Inexorably, digital and inside sales continue to take over many tasks that field salespeople used to do, especially for familiar purchases.

However, new and complex offerings still require salespeople who can identify perceived and latent needs, tailor solutions, and navigate complex buying organizations. Yes, AI will take tasks away from salespeople and narrow their role even more on complex situations. At the same time, the companies that sell AI technologies will create large sales forces to capture the looming massive and complex opportunities.

TAKEAWAYS

Generative AI can transform sales by freeing up time for sales representatives and managers to focus on more value-adding activities. When generative AI is properly integrated into sales processes, it is certain to increase productivity.

✓ These tools can assist in developing important account strategies, reversing administrative creep, providing personalized content and product offers, responding to proposal request emails, working with customers, and more.

✓ On the pathway to integrating these technologies, salespeople and sales managers will need strategies for dealing with inconsistency and inaccuracy, realizing value rapidly, and delivering results while controlling costs.

✓ AI is quickly becoming a necessary digital assistant, but for complex products, knowledgeable salespeople are and will continue to be needed.

Adapted from content posted on hbr.org, March 31, 2023 (product #H07JGX).

7

GENERATIVE AI HAS AN INTELLECTUAL PROPERTY PROBLEM

by Gil Appel, Juliana Neelbauer, and David A. Schweidel

Generative AI can seem like magic. Image generators such as Stable Diffusion, Midjourney, or DALL-E 2 can produce remarkable visuals in styles from aged photographs and watercolors to pencil drawings and pointillism. The resulting products can be fascinating—both quality and speed of creation are elevated compared with average human performance. The Museum of Modern Art in New York hosted an installation that was AI-generated from the museum's own collection, and the Mauritshuis in The Hague hung an AI variant of Vermeer's *Girl with a Pearl Earring* while the original was away on loan.

The capabilities of text generators are perhaps even more striking as they write essays, poems, and summaries and are proving adept mimics of style and form (though they can take creative license with facts).

While it may seem like these new AI tools can conjure new material from the ether, that's not quite the case. Generative AI platforms are trained on data lakes and question snippets—billions of parameters that are constructed by software processing huge archives of images and text. The AI platforms recover patterns and relationships, which they then use to create rules and then make judgments and predictions when responding to a prompt.

This process comes with legal risks, including intellectual property (IP) infringement. In many cases, it also poses legal questions that are still being resolved. For example, does copyright, patent, or trademark infringement apply to AI creations? Is it clear who owns the content that generative AI platforms create for you or your customers? Before businesses can embrace the benefits of generative AI, they need to understand the risks—and how to protect themselves.

Where Generative AI Fits into Today's Legal Landscape

Though generative AI may be new to the market, existing laws have significant implications for its use. Courts are sorting out how the laws on the books should be applied. There are infringement and right-of-use issues, uncertainty about ownership of AI-generated works, and questions about unlicensed content in training data and whether users should be able to prompt these tools with direct reference to other creators' copyrighted and trademarked works by name without their permission.

These claims are already being litigated. In a case filed in late 2022, *Andersen v. Stability AI et al.*, three artists formed a class to sue multiple generative AI platforms on the grounds that the AI was using their original works without license to train their AI in their styles. The platforms were thus allowing users to generate works that might be insufficiently transformative from the artists' existing protected works and, as a result, would be unauthorized derivative works. If a court finds that the AI's works are unauthorized and derivative, substantial infringement penalties can apply.

Similar cases filed in 2023 bring claims that companies trained AI tools using data lakes with thousands—or even many millions—of unlicensed works. Getty, an image licensing service, filed a lawsuit against the creators of Stable Diffusion alleging the improper use of its photos, violating both copyright and trademark rights it has in its watermarked photograph collection.

In each of these cases, the legal system is being asked to clarify the bounds of what is a "derivative work" under intellectual property laws—and depending on the jurisdiction, different federal circuit courts may respond with different interpretations. The outcome of these cases is expected to hinge on the interpretation of the fair use doctrine, which allows copyrighted work to be used without the owner's permission "for purposes such as criticism (including satire), comment, news reporting, teaching (including multiple copies for classroom use), scholarship, or research," and for a transformative use of the copyrighted material in a manner for which it was not intended.

This isn't the first time technology and copyright law have crashed into each other. Google successfully defended itself against a lawsuit by arguing that transformative use allowed for the scraping of text from books to create its search engine, and for the time being, this decision remains precedential.

But there are other, nontechnological cases that could shape how the products of generative AI are treated. A 2023 case before the U.S. Supreme Court against the Andy Warhol Foundation—brought by photographer Lynn Goldsmith, who had licensed an image of the late musician, Prince—may refine U.S. copyright law on the issue of when a piece of art is sufficiently different from its source material to become unequivocally "transformative" and whether a court can consider the meaning of the derivative work when it evaluates that transformation. The court's finding that the Warhol piece is not a fair use could mean trouble for AI-generated works.

All this uncertainty presents a slew of challenges for companies that use generative AI. There are risks regarding infringement—direct or unintentional—in contracts that are silent on generative AI usage by their vendors and customers. If a business user is aware that training data might include unlicensed works or that an AI can generate unauthorized derivative works not covered by fair use, a business could be on the hook for willful infringement, which can include damages up to $150,000 for each instance of knowing use. There's also the risk of accidentally sharing confidential trade secrets or business information by inputting data into generative AI tools.

Mitigating Risk and Building a Way Forward

This new paradigm means that companies need to take new steps to protect themselves for both the short and long term.

AI developers, for one, should ensure that they are in compliance with the law in regard to their acquisition of data being used to train their models. This should involve licensing and compensating those individuals who own the IP that developers seek to add to their training data, whether by licensing it or sharing in revenue generated by the AI tool. Customers of AI tools should ask providers whether their models were trained with any protected content, review the terms of service and privacy policies, and avoid generative AI tools that cannot confirm that their training data is properly licensed from content creators or subject to open-source licenses with which the AI companies comply.

Developers

In the long run, AI developers will need to take initiative about the ways they source their data—and investors need to know the origin of the data. Stable Diffusion,

Midjourney, and others have created their models based on the LAION-5B dataset, which contains almost 6 billion tagged images compiled from scraping the web indiscriminately and is known to include a substantial number of copyrighted creations.

Stability AI, which developed Stable Diffusion, has announced that artists will be able to opt out of the next generation of the image generator. But this puts the onus on content creators to actively protect their IP, rather than requiring the AI developers to secure the IP to the work prior to using it—and even when artists opt out, that decision will be reflected only in the next iteration of the platform. Instead, companies should require the creator's opt-in rather than opt-out.

Developers should also work on ways to maintain the provenance of AI-generated content, which would increase transparency about the works included in the training data. This would include recording the platform that was used to develop the content, details on the settings that were employed, tracking of seed data's metadata, and tags to facilitate AI reporting, including the generative seed and the specific prompt that was used to create the content. Such information would not only allow for the reproduction of the image, allowing its veracity to be verified easily, but it would also speak to the user's intent, thereby protecting business users that might need to overcome intellectual property infringement claims as well as demonstrate that the output was not due to willful intent to copy or steal.

Developing these audit trails would assure that companies are prepared if (or, more likely, when) customers start including demands for them in contracts as a form of insurance that the vendor's works aren't willfully, or unintentionally, derivative without authorization. Looking further into the future, insurance companies may require these reports in order to extend traditional insurance coverages to business users whose assets include AI-generated works. Breaking down the contributions of individual artists who were included in the training data to produce an image would further support efforts to appropriately compensate contributors, and even embed the copyright of the original artist in the new creation.

Creators

Both individual content creators and brands that create content should take steps to examine risks to their intellectual property portfolios and protect those portfolios. This involves proactively looking for their work in compiled datasets or large-scale data lakes, including visual elements such as logos and artwork as well as textual elements such as image tags. Obviously, this could not be done manually through terabytes or petabytes of content data, but existing search tools should allow the cost-effective automation of this task. New tools can even promise to obfuscate creators' works from being ingested into these algorithms.

Content creators should actively monitor digital and social channels for the appearance of works that may be derived from their own. For brands with valuable trademarks to protect, it's not simply a matter of looking for specific elements such as the Nike Swoosh or Tiffany Blue. Rather, there may be a need for trademark and trade dress (the general appearance of a product, including both its design and its packaging) monitoring to evolve in order to examine the style of derivative works, which may have arisen from being trained on a specific set of a brand's images. Even though critical elements such as a logo or specific color may not be present in an AI-generated image, other stylistic elements may suggest that salient elements of a brand's content were used to produce a derivative work. Such similarities may suggest the intent to appropriate the average consumer's goodwill for the brand by using recognizable visual or auditory elements. Mimicry may be seen as the sincerest form of flattery, but it can also suggest the purposeful misuse of a brand.

The good news regarding trademark infringement for business owners is that trademark attorneys have well-established protocols for how to notify and enforce trademark rights against an infringer, such as by sending a strongly worded cease-and-desist notice or licensing demand letter, or moving directly to filing a trademark infringement claim, regardless of whether an AI platform or a human generated the unauthorized branding.

Businesses

Businesses should evaluate their transaction terms to write protections into contracts. As a starting point, they should demand terms of service from generative AI platforms that confirm proper licensure of the training data that feeds their AI. They should also demand broad indemnification for potential intellectual property infringement caused by a failure of the AI companies to properly license data input or self-reporting by the AI itself of its outputs to flag for potential infringement.

At a minimum, if either party is using generative AI, businesses should add disclosures in their vendor and customer agreements (for custom services and products delivery) to ensure that intellectual property rights are understood and protected on both sides of the table. They should also disclose how each party will support registration of authorship and ownership of those works. Vendor and customer contracts can include AI-related language added to confidentiality provisions to bar receiving parties from inputting confidential information of the information-disclosing parties into text prompts of AI tools.

To reduce unintended risks of use, some leading firms have created generative AI checklists for contract modifications for their clients that assess each clause for AI implications. Organizations that use generative AI, or work with vendors that do, should keep their legal counsel abreast of the scope and nature of that use as the law will continue to evolve rapidly.

. . .

Going forward, content creators that have a sufficient library of their own intellectual property on which to draw may consider building their own datasets to train and mature AI platforms. The resulting generative AI models need not be trained from scratch but can build on open-source generative AI that has used lawfully sourced content. This would enable content creators to produce content in the same style as their own work with an audit trail to their own data lake or to license the use of such tools to interested parties with cleared title in both the AI's training data and its outputs. In this same spirit, content creators who have developed an online following may consider co-creation with followers as another means by which to source training data, recognizing that these co-creators should be asked for their permission to make use of their content in terms of service and privacy policies that are updated as the law changes.

Generative AI will change the nature of content creation, enabling many to do what, until now, only a few had the skills or advanced technology to accomplish at high speed. As this burgeoning technology develops, users must respect the rights of those who have enabled its creation—those very content creators who may be displaced by it. And while we understand the real threat of generative AI to be part of the livelihood of members of the creative class, it also poses a risk to brands that have used visuals to meticulously craft their identity. At the same time, both creatives and corporate interests have a dramatic opportunity to build portfolios of their works and branded materials, meta-tag them, and train their own generative AI platforms that can produce authorized, proprietary (paid-up or royalty-bearing) goods as sources of instant revenue streams.

TAKEAWAYS

Generative AI, which uses data lakes and question snippets to recover patterns and relationships, is becoming more prevalent in creative industries. However, the legal implications of using generative AI are still unclear, particularly in relation to copyright infringement, ownership of AI-generated works, and unlicensed content in training data.

✓ Courts are currently trying to establish how intellectual property laws should be applied to generative AI, and several cases have already been filed.

✓ To protect themselves from unintentionally violating copyright laws, companies that use generative AI need to ensure that they are in compliance with the law and take steps to mitigate potential risks, such as ensuring they use training data free from unlicensed content and developing ways to show provenance of generated content.

✓ Both individual content creators and brands that create content should take steps to examine risks to their intellectual property portfolios and protect those assets.

Adapted from content posted on hbr.org, April 7, 2023 (product #H07K15).

8

AI PROMPT ENGINEERING ISN'T THE FUTURE

by Oguz A. Acar

Prompt engineering has taken the generative AI world by storm. The job, which entails optimizing textual input to effectively communicate with large language models, has been hailed by the World Economic Forum as the number one "job of the future," while OpenAI CEO Sam Altman characterized it as an "amazingly high-leveraged skill." Social media brims with a new wave of influencers showcasing "magic prompts" and pledging amazing outcomes.

However, despite the buzz surrounding it, the prominence of prompt engineering may be fleeting for several reasons. First, future generations of AI systems will get more intuitive and adept at understanding natural language, reducing the need for meticulously engineered prompts. Second, new AI language models like GPT-4 already show great promise in crafting prompts—AI itself is on the verge of rendering prompt engineering obsolete. Lastly, the efficacy of prompts is contingent on the specific algorithm, limiting their utility across diverse AI models and versions.

So, what is a more enduring and adaptable skill that will keep enabling us to harness the potential of generative AI? It is *problem formulation*—the ability to identify, analyze, and delineate problems.

Problem formulation and prompt engineering differ in their focus, core tasks, and underlying abilities. Prompt engineering focuses on crafting the optimal textual input by selecting the appropriate words, phrases, sentence structures, and punctuation. In contrast, problem formulation emphasizes defining the problem by delineating its focus, scope, and boundaries. Prompt engineering requires a firm grasp of a specific AI tool and linguistic proficiency, while problem formulation necessitates a comprehensive understanding of the problem domain and ability to distill real-world issues. The fact is, without a well-formulated problem, even the most sophisticated prompts will fall short. However, once a problem is clearly defined, the linguistics nuances of a prompt become tangential to the solution.

Unfortunately, problem formulation is a widely overlooked and underdeveloped skill for most of us. One reason is the disproportionate emphasis given to problem-solving at the expense of formulation. This imbalance is perhaps best illustrated by the prevalent yet misguided management adage, "Don't bring me problems. Bring me solutions." It is therefore not surprising to see a survey revealing that 85% of C-suite executives consider their organizations bad at diagnosing problems.[1]

How can you get better at problem formulation? By synthesizing insights from past research on problem formulation and job design as well as my own experience and research on crowdsourcing platforms—where organizational challenges are regularly articulated and opened up to large audiences—I have identified four key components for effective problem formulation: *problem diagnosis, decomposition, reframing,* and *constraint design.*

Problem Diagnosis

Problem diagnosis is about identifying the core problem for AI to solve. In other words, it concerns identifying the main objective you want generative AI to accomplish. Some problems are relatively simple to pinpoint, such as when the objective is gaining information on a specific topic like various human resources management strategies for employee compensation. Others are more challenging, such as then exploring solutions to an innovation problem.

A case in point is InnoCentive (now Wazoku Crowd). The company has helped its clients formulate more than 2,500 problems, with an impressive success rate over 80%. My interviews with InnoCentive employees revealed that a key factor behind this success was their ability to discern the fundamental issue underlying a problem. In fact, they often start their problem formulation process by using the "Five Whys" technique to distinguish the root causes from mere symptoms.

A particular instance is the problem of cleaning up subarctic waters after the catastrophic *Exxon Valdez* oil spill. Collaborating with the Oil Spill Recovery Institute, InnoCentive pinpointed the root cause of the oil cleanup issue as the viscosity of the crude oil: The frozen oil became too thick to pump from barges. This diagnosis was key to finally cracking the two-decade-old problem with a solution that involved using a modified version of construction equipment designed to vibrate the oil, keeping it in a liquid state.

Problem Decomposition

Problem decomposition entails breaking down complex problems into smaller, manageable subproblems. This is particularly important when you are tackling multifaceted problems, which are often too convoluted to generate useful solutions.

Take the InnoCentive amyotrophic lateral sclerosis (ALS) challenge, for example. Rather than seeking solutions for the broad problem of discovering a treatment for ALS, the challenge concentrated on a subcomponent of it: detecting and monitoring the progress of the disease. Consequently, an ALS biomarker was developed for the first time, providing a noninvasive and cost-efficient solution based on measuring electrical current flow through muscle tissue.

I tested how AI improves with problem decomposition using a timely and common organizational challenge: implementing a robust cybersecurity framework. Bing's AI-powered solutions were too broad and generic to be immediately useful. But after breaking it down into subproblems—e.g., security policies, vulnerability assessments, authentication protocols, and employee training—the solutions improved considerably. The cases discussed below illustrate the difference. Methods such as functional decomposition or work breakdown structure can help you visually depict complex problems and simplify the identification of individual components and their interconnections that are most relevant for your organization.

Problem Reframing

Problem reframing involves changing the perspective from which a problem is viewed, enabling alternative interpretations. By reframing a problem in various ways, you can guide AI to broaden the scope of potential solutions, which can, in turn, help you find optimal solutions and overcome creative roadblocks.

Consider Doug Dietz, an innovation architect at GE HealthCare, whose main responsibility was designing state-of-the-art MRI scanners. During a hospital visit, he saw a terrified child awaiting an MRI scan and discovered that a staggering 80% of children needed sedation to cope with the intimidating experience. This revelation prompted him to reframe the problem: "How can we turn the daunting MRI experience into an exciting adventure for kids?" This fresh angle led to the development of the GE Adventure Series, which dramatically lowered pediatric sedation rates to a mere 15%, increased patient satisfaction scores by 90%, and improved machine efficiency.

Now imagine this: Employees are complaining about the lack of available parking spaces at the office building. The initial framing may focus on increasing parking space, but by reframing the problem from the employees' perspective—finding parking stressful or having limited commuting options—you can explore different solutions. Indeed, when I asked ChatGPT to generate solutions for the parking space problem using initial and alternative frames, the former yielded solutions centered on optimizing parking layouts or allocation and finding new spaces. The latter produced a diverse solution set such as promoting alternative transportation, sustainable commuting, and remote work.

To effectively reframe problems, consider taking the perspective of users, exploring analogies to represent the problem, using abstraction, and proactively questioning problem objectives or identifying missing components in the problem definition.

Problem Constraint Design

Problem constraint design focuses on delineating the boundaries of a problem by defining input, process, and output restrictions of the solution search. You can use constraints to direct AI in generating solutions valuable for the task at hand. When the task is primarily productivity-oriented, employing specific and strict constraints to outline the context, boundaries, and outcome criteria is often more appropriate. In contrast, for creativity-oriented tasks, experimenting with imposing, modifying, and removing constraints allows exploring a wider solution space and discovering novel perspectives.

For example, brand managers are already using several AI tools, such as Lately or Jasper, to produce useful social media content at scale. To ensure this content is aligned with different media and brand image, they are often setting precise constraints on the length, format, tone, or target audience.

When seeking true originality, however, brand managers can eliminate formatting constraints or restraining the output to an unconventional format. A great example is GoFundMe's Help Changes Everything campaign. The company aimed to generate year-in-review creative content that would not only express gratitude to its donors and evoke emotions but also stand out from the typical year-end content. To accomplish this, it set unorthodox constraints: The visuals would rely exclusively on AI-generated street mural–style art and feature all fundraising campaigns and donors. DALL-E and Stable

Diffusion generated individual images that were then transformed into an emotionally charged video. The result: a visually cohesive and striking aesthetic that garnered widespread acclaim.[2]

. . .

Overall, honing skills in problem diagnosis, decomposition, reframing, and constraint design is essential for aligning AI outcomes with task objectives and fostering effective collaboration with AI systems.

Although prompt engineering may hold the spotlight in the short term, its lack of sustainability, versatility, and transferability limits its long-term relevance. Overemphasizing the crafting of the perfect combination of words can even be counterproductive, as it may detract from the exploration of the problem itself and diminish the user's sense of control over the creative process. Instead, mastering problem formulation could be the key to navigating the uncertain future alongside sophisticated AI systems. It might prove to be as pivotal as learning programming languages was during the early days of computing.

TAKEAWAYS

Despite the buzz surrounding prompt engineering, its prominence may be fleeting. Problem formulation—the ability to identify, analyze, and delineate problems—will be a more enduring and adaptable skill that will continue to enable us to harness the potential of generative AI:

✓ Problem formulation involves four components: problem diagnosis, decomposition, reframing, and constraint design—and it necessitates a thorough understanding of the problem domain.

✓ Due to the increasing sophistication of AI, mastering problem formulation may become as important as learning programming languages was in the early days of computing.

NOTES

1. Thomas Wedell-Wedellsborg, "Are You Solving the Right Problems?," *Harvard Business Review*, January–February 2017, https://hbr.org/2017/01/are-you-solving-the-right-problems.

2. Audrey Kemp, "US Ad of the Day: GoFundMe Paints the Power of Donating in 'The Bigger Picture,'" *Drum*, December 21, 2022, https://www.thedrum.com/news/2022/12/21/us-ad-the-day -gofundme-paints-the-power-donating-the-bigger-picture.

Adapted from content posted on hbr.org, June 6, 2023 (product #H07NQK).

9

EIGHT QUESTIONS ABOUT USING AI RESPONSIBLY, ANSWERED

by Tsedal Neeley

W hile the question of how organizations can (and should) use AI isn't a new one, the stakes and urgency of finding answers have skyrocketed with the release of ChatGPT, Midjourney, and other generative AI tools. Everywhere, people are wondering: *How can we use AI tools to boost performance? Can we trust*

AI to make consequential decisions? Will AI take away my job?

The power of AI introduced by OpenAI, Microsoft, and NVIDIA—and the pressure to compete in the market—makes it inevitable that your organization will have to navigate the operational and ethical considerations of machine learning, large language models, and much more. And while many leaders are focused on operational challenges and disruptions, the ethical concerns are at least as—if not more—pressing. Given how regulation lags technological capabilities and how quickly the AI landscape is changing, the burden of ensuring that these tools are used safely and ethically falls to companies.

In my work at the intersection of occupations, technology, and organizations, I've examined how leaders can develop digital mindsets and the dangers of biased large language models. I have identified best practices for organizations' use of technology and amplified consequential issues that ensure that AI implementations are ethical. To help you better identify how you and your company should be thinking about these issues—and make no mistake, you *should* be thinking about them—I collaborated with HBR to answer eight questions posed by readers on LinkedIn.

1. How should I prepare to introduce AI at my organization?

To start, it's important to recognize that the optimal way to work with AI is different from the way we've worked with other new technologies. In the past, most new tools simply enabled us to perform tasks more efficiently. People wrote with pens, then typewriters (which were faster), then computers (which were even faster). Each new tool allowed for more efficient writing, but the general processes (drafting, revising, editing) remained largely the same.

AI is different. It has a more substantial influence on our work and our processes because it's able to find patterns that we can't see and then use them to provide insights and analysis, predictions, suggestions, and even full drafts all on its own. So instead of thinking of AI as the tools we use, we should think of it as a set of *systems* with which we can collaborate.

To effectively collaborate with AI at your organization, focus on three things:

First, ensure that everyone has a basic understanding of how digital systems work

A digital mindset is a collection of attitudes and behaviors that help you see new possibilities using data, technology, algorithms, and AI. You don't have to become a programmer or a data scientist; you simply need to take a new and proactive approach to collaboration (learning to work across platforms), computation (asking and answering the right questions), and change (accepting that it is the only constant). *Everyone* in your organization should be working toward at least 30% fluency in a handful of topics, such as systems architecture, AI, machine learning, algorithms, AI agents as teammates, cybersecurity, and data-driven experimentation.[1]

Second, make sure your organization is prepared for continuous adaptation and change

Bringing in new AI requires employees to get used to processing new streams of data and content, analyzing them, and using their findings and outputs to develop a different perspective. Likewise, to use data and technology most efficiently, organizations need an integrated organizational structure. Your company needs to become less siloed and should build a centralized repository of knowledge and data to enable constant sharing and collaboration. Competing with AI requires not only incorporating today's technologies but also being mentally and structurally prepared to adapt to future advancements. For example, individuals have begun incorporating generative AI (such as ChatGPT) into their daily routines, regardless of whether companies are prepared or willing to embrace its use.

Third, build AI into your operating model

As my colleagues Marco Iansiti and Karim R. Lakhani showed in their book *Competing in the Age of AI*, the structure of an organization mirrors the architecture of the technological systems within it, and vice versa. If tech systems are static, your organization will be static. But if they're flexible, your organization will be flexible. This strategy played out successfully at Amazon. The company was having trouble sustaining its growth and its software infrastructure was "cracking under pressure," according to Iansiti and Lakhani. So Jeff Bezos wrote a memo to employees announcing that all teams should route their data through APIs, which allow various types of software to communicate and share data using set protocols. Anyone who didn't would be fired. This was an attempt to break the inertia within Amazon's tech systems—and it worked, dismantling data siloes, increasing collaboration, and helping to build the software- and data-driven operating model we see today. While you may not want to resort to a similar ultimatum, you should think about how the introduction of AI can—and should—change your operations for the better.

2. How can we ensure transparency in how AI makes decisions?

Leaders need to recognize that it is not always possible to know how AI systems are making decisions. Some of the very characteristics that allow AI to quickly process huge amounts of data and perform certain tasks more accurately or efficiently than humans can also make it a black box: We can't see how the output was produced. However, we can all play a role in increasing transparency and accountability in AI decision-making processes in two ways:

Recognize that AI is invisible and inscrutable and be transparent in presenting and using AI systems

Callen Anthony, Beth A. Bechky, and Anne-Laure Fayard identify invisibility and inscrutability as core characteristics that differentiate AI from prior technologies.[2] It's invisible because it often runs in the background of other technologies or platforms without users being aware of it; for every Siri or Alexa that people understand to be AI, there are many technologies, such as antilock brakes, that contain unseen AI systems. It's inscrutable because, even for AI developers, it's often impossible to understand how a model reaches an outcome, or even identify all the data points it's using to get there—good, bad, or otherwise.

As AIs rely on progressively larger datasets, this becomes increasingly true. Consider large language models (LLMs) such as OpenAI's ChatGPT or Microsoft's Bing. They are trained on massive datasets of books, web pages, and documents scraped from across the internet—OpenAI's LLM was trained using *175 billion parameters* and was built to predict the *likelihood* that something would occur (a character, word, or string of words, or even an image or tonal shift in the user's voice) based on either its preceding or surrounding context. The autocorrect feature on your phone is an example of the accuracy—and inaccuracy—of such predictions. But it's not just the size of the training data: Many AI algorithms are also self-learning; they keep refining their predictive powers as they get more data and user feedback, adding new parameters along the way.

AIs often have broad capabilities *because* of invisibility and inscrutability—their ability to work in the background and find patterns beyond our grasp. Currently, there is no way to peer into the inner workings of an AI tool and guarantee that the system is producing accurate or fair output. We must acknowledge that some opacity is a cost of using these powerful systems. As a consequence, leaders should exercise careful judgment in determining when and how it's appropriate to use AI, and they should document when and how AI is being used. That way people will know that an AI-driven decision was appraised with an appropriate level of skepticism, including its potential risks or shortcomings.

Prioritize explanation as a central design goal

A 2020 research brief by MIT scientists notes that AI models can become more transparent through practices like highlighting specific areas in data that contribute to AI output, building models that are more interpretable, and developing algorithms that can be used to probe how a different model works.[3] Similarly, leading AI computer scientist Timnit Gebru and her colleagues Emily M. Bender, Angelina McMillan-Major, and Margaret Mitchell (credited as "Shmargaret Shmitchell") argue that practices like premortem analyses that prompt developers to consider both project risks and potential alternatives to current plans can increase transparency in future technologies.[4] Echoing this point, in March 2023, prominent tech entrepreneurs Steve Wozniak and Elon Musk, along with employees of Google and Microsoft, signed a letter advocating for AI development to be more transparent and interpretable.

3. How can we erect guardrails around LLMs so that their responses are true and consistent with the brand image we want to project?

LLMs come with several serious risks. They can:

- **Perpetuate harmful bias** by deploying negative stereotypes or minimizing minority viewpoints

- **Spread misinformation** by repeating falsehoods or making up facts and citations

- **Violate privacy** by using data without people's consent

- **Cause security breaches** if they are used to generate phishing emails or other cyberattacks

- **Harm the environment** because of the significant computational resources required to train and run them

Data curation and documentation are two ways to curtail those risks and ensure that LLMs will give responses that are more consistent with—not harmful to—your brand image.

Tailor data for appropriate outputs

LLMs are often developed using internet-based data containing billions of words. However, common sources of this data, like Reddit and Wikipedia, lack sufficient mechanisms for checking accuracy, fairness, or appropriateness. Consider which perspectives are represented on these sites and which are left out. For example, 67% of Reddit's contributors are male.[5] And on Wikipedia, 84% of contributors are male, with little representation from marginalized populations.[6]

If you instead build an LLM around more carefully vetted sources, you reduce the risk of inappropriate or harmful responses. Bender and colleagues recommend curating training datasets "through a thoughtful process of deciding what to put in, rather than aiming solely for scale and trying haphazardly to weed out ... 'dangerous,' 'unintelligible,' or 'otherwise bad' [data]."[7] While this might take more time and resources, it exemplifies the adage that an ounce of prevention is worth a pound of cure.

Document data

There will surely be organizations that want to leverage LLMs but lack the resources to train a model with a curated dataset. In situations like this, documentation is crucial because it enables companies to get context from a nonproprietary model's developers on which datasets it uses and the biases they may contain, as well as guidance on how software built on the model might be appropriately deployed. This practice is analogous to the standardized information used in medicine to indicate which studies have been used in making health-care recommendations.

AI developers should prioritize documentation to allow for safe and transparent use of their models. And people or organizations experimenting with a model must look for this documentation to understand its risks and whether it aligns with their desired brand image.

4. How can we ensure that the dataset we use to train AI models is representative and doesn't include harmful biases?

Sanitizing datasets is a challenge that your organization can help overcome by prioritizing transparency and fairness over model size and by representing diverse populations in data curation.

First, consider the trade-offs you make. Tech companies have been pursuing larger AI systems because they tend to be more effective at certain tasks, like sustaining human-seeming conversations. However, if a model is too large to fully understand, it's impossible to rid it of potential biases. To fully combat harmful bias, developers must be able to understand and document the risks inherent to a dataset, which might mean using a smaller one.

Second, if diverse teams, including members of underrepresented populations, collect and produce the data used to train models, you'll have a better chance of ensuring that people with a variety of perspectives and identities are represented in them. This practice also helps identify unrecognized biases or blinders in the data.

AI will only be trustworthy once it works equitably, and that will happen only if we prioritize diversifying data and development teams and clearly document how AI has been designed for fairness.

5. What are the potential risks of data privacy violations with AI?

AI that uses sensitive employee and customer data is vulnerable to bad actors. To combat these risks, organizations should learn as much as they can about how their AI has been developed and then decide whether it's appropriate to use secure data with it. They should also keep tech systems updated and earmark budget resources to keep the software secure. This requires continuous action, as a small vulnerability can leave an entire organization open to breaches.

Blockchain innovations can help on this front. A blockchain is a secure, distributed ledger that records data transactions, and it's currently being used for applications like creating payment systems (not to mention cryptocurrencies).

When it comes to your operations more broadly, consider this privacy by design (PbD) framework from former information and privacy commissioner of Ontario Ann Cavoukian, which recommends that organizations embrace seven foundational principles:

- Be proactive, not reactive—preventive, not remedial.

- Lead with privacy as the default setting.

- Embed privacy into design.

- Retain full functionality, including privacy and security.

- Ensure end-to-end security.

- Maintain visibility and transparency.

- Respect user privacy—keep systems user-centric.[8]

Incorporating PbD principles into your operation requires more than hiring privacy personnel or creating a privacy division. All the people in your organization need to be attuned to customer and employee concerns about these issues. Privacy isn't an afterthought; it needs to be at the core of digital operations, and everyone needs to work to protect it.

6. How can we encourage employees to use AI for productivity purposes and not simply to take shortcuts?

Even with the advent of LLMs, AI technology is not yet capable of performing the dizzying range of tasks that humans can, and there are many things that it does worse than the average person. Using each new tool effectively requires understanding its purpose.

For example, think about ChatGPT. By learning about language patterns, it has become so good at predicting which words are supposed to follow others that it can produce seemingly sophisticated text responses to complicated questions. However, there's a limit to the quality of these outputs because being good at guessing plausible combinations of words and phrases is different from understanding the material. So ChatGPT can produce a poem in the style of Shakespeare because it has learned the particular patterns of his plays and poems, but it cannot produce the original insight into the human condition that informs his work.

By contrast, AI can be better and more efficient than humans at making predictions because it can process much larger amounts of data much more quickly. Examples include predicting early dementia from speech patterns, detecting cancerous tumors indistinguishable to the human eye, and planning safer routes through battlefields.

Employees should therefore be encouraged to evaluate whether AI's strengths match up to a task and proceed accordingly. If you need to process a lot of information quickly, it can do that. If you need a bunch of new ideas, it can generate them. Even if you need to make a difficult decision, it can offer advice, providing it's been trained on relevant data.

But you shouldn't use AI to create meaningful work products without human oversight. If you need to write a quantity of documents with very similar content, AI may be a useful generator of what has long been referred to as "boilerplate" material. But be aware that its outputs are derived from its datasets and algorithms, and they aren't necessarily good or accurate.

7. How worried should we be that AI will replace jobs?

Every technological revolution has created more jobs than it has destroyed. Automobiles put horse-and-buggy drivers out of business but led to new jobs building and fixing cars, running gas stations, and more. The novelty of AI technologies makes it easy to fear they will replace humans in the workforce. But we should instead view them as ways to augment human performance. For example, companies like Collective[i] have developed AI systems that analyze data to produce highly accurate sales forecasts quickly; traditionally, this work took people days or weeks to pull together. But no salespeople are losing their jobs. Rather, they've got more time to focus on more important parts of their work: building relationships, managing, and actually selling.

Similarly, services like OpenAI's Codex can autogenerate programming code for basic purposes. This doesn't replace programmers; it allows them to write code more efficiently and automate repetitive tasks like testing so that they can work on higher-level issues such as systems architecture, domain modeling, and user experience.

The long-term effects on jobs are complex and uneven, and there can be periods of job destruction and displacement in certain industries or regions. To ensure that the benefits of technological progress are widely shared, it is crucial to invest in education and workforce development to help people adapt to the new job market.

Individuals and organizations should focus on upskilling and scaling to prepare to make the most of new technologies. AI and robots aren't replacing humans anytime soon. The more likely reality is that people with digital mindsets will replace those without them.

8. How can my organization ensure that the AI we develop or use won't harm individuals or groups or violate human rights?

The harms of AI bias have been widely documented. In their seminal 2018 paper "Gender Shades," Joy Buolamwini and Timnit Gebru showed that popular facial recognition technologies offered by companies like IBM and Microsoft were nearly perfect at identifying white male faces but misidentified Black female faces as much as 35% of the time.[9] Facial recognition can be used to unlock your phone but is also used to monitor patrons at Madison Square Garden, surveil protesters, and tap suspects in police investigations—and misidentification has led to wrongful arrests that can derail people's lives. As AI grows in power and becomes more integrated into our daily lives, its potential for harm grows exponentially, too. Here are strategies to safeguard AI.

Slow down and document AI development

Preventing AI harm requires shifting our focus from the rapid development and deployment of increasingly powerful AI to ensuring that AI is safe before release.

Transparency is also key. Earlier in this article, I explained how clear descriptions of the datasets used in AI and potential biases within them helps reduce harm. When algorithms are openly shared, organizations and individuals can better analyze and understand the potential risks of new tools before using them.

Establish and protect AI ethics watchdogs

The question of who will ensure safe and responsible AI is currently unanswered. Google, for example, employs an ethical-AI team, but in 2020 the company fired Gebru after she sought to publish a paper warning of the risks of building ever-larger language models. Her exit from Google raised the question of whether tech developers are able, or incentivized, to act as ombudsmen for their own technologies and organizations. More recently, an entire team at Microsoft focused on ethics was laid off.[10] But many in the industry recognize the risks, and as noted earlier, even tech icons have called for policy makers working with technologists to create regulatory systems to govern AI development.

Whether it comes from government, the tech industry, or another independent system, the establishment and protection of watchdogs is crucial to protecting against AI harm.

Watch where regulation is headed

Even as the AI landscape changes, governments are trying to regulate it. In the United States, 21 AI-related bills were passed into law last year. Notable acts include an Alabama provision outlining guidelines for using facial recognition technology in criminal proceedings and legislation in Vermont that created a Division of Artificial Intelligence to review all AI used by the state government and to propose a state AI code of ethics. In early 2023, the U.S. federal government moved to enact executive actions on AI, which will be vetted over time.

The European Union is also considering legislation—the Artificial Intelligence Act—that includes a classification system determining the level of risk AI could pose to the health and safety or the fundamental rights of a person. Italy has temporarily banned ChatGPT. The African Union has established a working group on AI, and the African Commission on Human and Peoples' Rights adopted a resolution to address implications for human rights of AI, robotics, and other new and emerging technologies in Africa.

China passed a data protection law in 2021 that established user consent rules for data collection and recently passed a unique policy regulating "deep synthesis technologies" that are used for so-called deep fakes. The British government released an approach that applies existing regulatory guidelines to new AI technology.

. . .

Billions of people around the world are discovering the promise of AI through their experiments with ChatGPT, Bing, Midjourney, and other new tools. Every company will have to confront questions about how these emerging technologies will apply to them and their industries. For some it will mean a significant pivot in their operating models; for others, an opportunity to scale and broaden their offerings. But all must assess their readiness to deploy AI responsibly without perpetuating harm to their stakeholders and the world at large.

TAKEAWAYS

Generative AI tools are poised to change the way every business operates. As your own organization begins strategizing about which to use and how, operational and ethical considerations are inevitable. This article delves into eight of them:

✓ How should I prepare to introduce AI at my organization?

✓ How can we ensure transparency in how AI makes decisions?

✓ How can we erect guardrails around LLMs so that their responses are true and consistent with the brand image we want to project?

✓ How can we ensure that the dataset we use to train AI models is representative and doesn't include harmful biases?

✓ What are the potential risks of data privacy violations with AI?

✓ How can we encourage employees to use AI for productivity purposes and not simply to take shortcuts?

✓ How worried should we be that AI will replace jobs?

✓ How can my organization ensure that the AI we develop or use won't harm individuals or groups or violate human rights?

NOTES

1. Tsedal Neely, "Developing a Digital Mindset by Following the 30% Rule," LinkedIn, May 12, 2022, https://www.linkedin.com /pulse/developing-digital-mindset-following-30-rule-tsedal-neeley/.

2. Callen Anthony, Beth A. Bechky, and Anne-Laure Fayard, "'Collaborating' with AI: Taking a System View to Explore the Future of Work," *Organization Science*, January 9, 2023, https://pubsonline.informs.org/doi/abs/10.1287/orsc.2022.1651 ?journalCode=orsc.

3. Thomas W. Malone, Daniela Rus, and Robert Laubacher, "Artificial Intelligence and the Future of Work," MIT Research Brief 17 (December 2020), https://workofthefuture.mit.edu/wp -content/uploads/2020/12/2020-Research-Brief-Malone-Rus -Laubacher2.pdf.

4. Emily M. Bender, Timnit Gebru, Angelina McMillan-Major, and Shmargaret Shmitchell, "On the Dangers of Stochastic Parrots: Can Language Models Be Too Big?," *Proceedings of the 2021 ACM Conference on Fairness, Accountability, and Transparency*, FAccT '21, New York, NY, March 2021, https://dl.acm.org/doi/10 .1145/3442188.3445922.

5. Robert M. Bond and R. Kelly Garrett, "Engagement with Fact-Checked Posts on Reddit," *PNAS Nexus* 2, no. 3 (March 2023), https://academic.oup.com/pnasnexus/article/2/3/pgad018/7008465.

6. "Community Insights 2021 Report, Thriving Movement," Wikimedia Meta-Wiki, https://meta.m.wikimedia.org/wiki /Community_Insights/Community_Insights_2021_Report /Thriving_Movement#Community_and_Newcomer_Diversity.

7. Bender et al., "On the Dangers of Stochastic Parrots."

8. Ann Cavoukian, "Privacy by Design: the 7 Foundational Principles," privacybydesign.ca, January 2011, https://www.ipc.on .ca/wp-content/uploads/Resources/7foundationalprinciples.pdf.

9. Joy Buolamwini and Timnit Gebru, "Gender Shades: Intersectional Accuracy Disparities in Commercial Gender Classification," *Proceedings of the 1st Conference on Fairness, Accountability and Transparency, PMLR* 81 (2018): 77–91, https://proceedings.mlr .press/v81/buolamwini18a.html.

10. Rebecca Bellan, "Microsoft Lays Off an Ethical AI Team as It Doubles Down on OpenAI," TechCrunch, March 13, 2023, https:// techcrunch.com/2023/03/13/microsoft-lays-off-an-ethical-ai-team -as-it-doubles-down-on-openai/.

Adapted from content posted on hbr.org, May 9, 2023 (product #H07MEI).

10

MANAGING THE RISKS OF GENERATIVE AI

by Kathy Baxter and Yoav Schlesinger

C orporate leaders, academics, policy makers, and countless others are looking for ways to harness generative AI technology. In business, generative AI has the potential to transform the way companies interact with customers and drive business growth. New research shows 67% of senior IT leaders are prioritizing generative AI for their business within the next 18 months, with one-third (33%) naming it as a top priority, and companies are exploring how it could impact every part of the business.[1]

Senior IT leaders need a trusted, data-secure way for their employees to use these technologies. Seventy-nine percent of these leaders reported concerns that these technologies bring the potential for security risks, and another 73% are concerned about biased outcomes. More broadly, organizations must recognize the need to ensure the ethical, transparent, and responsible use of these technologies.

A business using generative AI technology in an enterprise setting is different from consumers using it for private, individual use. Businesses need to adhere to regulations relevant to their respective industries (think health care), and there's a minefield of legal, financial, and ethical implications if the content generated is inaccurate, inaccessible, or offensive. For example, the risk of harm when a generative AI chatbot gives incorrect steps for cooking a recipe is much lower than when giving a field-service worker instructions for repairing a piece of heavy machinery. If not designed and deployed with clear ethical guidelines, generative AI can have unintended consequences and potentially cause real harm.

Organizations need a clear and actionable framework for how to use generative AI and to align their generative AI goals with their businesses' "jobs to be done," including how generative AI will impact sales, marketing, commerce, service, and IT jobs.

In 2019, we at Salesforce published our trusted principles (transparency, fairness, responsibility, accountability, and reliability), meant to guide the development of ethical AI tools. These can apply to any organization investing in AI. But these principles only go so far if organizations lack an ethical AI practice to operationalize them into the development and adoption of AI technology. A mature ethical AI practice operationalizes its principles or values through responsible product development and deployment—uniting disciplines such as product management, data science, engineering, privacy, legal, user research, design, and accessibility—to mitigate AI's potential harms and maximize its social benefits. There are models for how organizations can start, mature, and expand these practices; these models provide clear road maps for how to build the infrastructure for ethical AI development.[2]

But with the mainstream emergence—and accessibility—of generative AI, we recognized that organizations needed guidelines specific to the risks this technology presents. These guidelines don't replace our principles, but instead act as a North Star for how they can be operationalized and put into practice as businesses develop products and services that use this new technology.

Guidelines for the Ethical Development of Generative AI

Our new set of guidelines can help organizations evaluate generative AI's risks and considerations as these tools gain mainstream adoption. They cover five focus areas.

Accuracy

Organizations need to be able to train AI models on their own data to deliver verifiable results that balance accuracy, precision, and recall (the model's ability to correctly identify positive cases within a given dataset). It's important to communicate when there is uncertainty regarding generative AI responses and enable people to validate them. This can be done by citing the sources of information the model is using to create content, explaining why the AI gave the response it did, highlighting uncertainty, and creating guardrails that prevent some tasks from being fully automated.

Safety

Making every effort to mitigate bias, toxicity, and harmful outputs by conducting bias, explainability, and robustness assessments is always a priority in AI. Organizations must protect the privacy of any personally identifying information in the data used for training to prevent potential harm. Further, security assessments can help organizations identify vulnerabilities that may be exploited by bad actors.

Honesty

When collecting data to train and evaluate our models, respect data provenance and ensure there is consent to use that data. This can be done by leveraging open-source and user-provided data. And, when autonomously delivering outputs, it's necessary to be transparent that an AI has created the content. This can be done through watermarks on the content or through in-app messaging.

Empowerment

While there are some cases where it is best to fully automate processes, AI should more often play a supporting role. Today, generative AI is a great *assistant*. In industries where building trust is a top priority, such as in finance or health care, it's important that humans be involved in decision-making—with the help of data-driven insights that an AI model may provide—to build trust and maintain transparency. Additionally, ensure the model's outputs are accessible to all (e.g., generate alt text to accompany images, text output is accessible to a screen reader). And of course, one must treat content contributors, creators, and data labelers with respect (e.g., fair wages, consent to use their work).

Sustainability

Language models are described as "large" based on the number of values or parameters they use. Some of these large language models have hundreds of billions of parameters, and it takes a lot of energy and water to train them. For example, GPT-3 took 1.287 gigawatt hours, or about as much electricity to power 120 U.S. homes for a year, and 700,000 liters of clean fresh water.[3]

When considering AI models, larger doesn't always mean better. As we develop our own models, we will strive to minimize the size of our models while maximizing accuracy by training on models on large amounts of high-quality CRM data. This will help reduce the carbon footprint because less computation is required, which means less energy consumption from data centers and carbon emission.

Integrating Generative AI

Most organizations will integrate generative AI tools rather than build their own. Here are some tactical tips for safely integrating generative AI in business applications to drive business results:

Use zero-party or first-party data

Companies should train generative AI tools using zero-party data—data that customers share proactively—and first-party data, which they collect directly. Strong data provenance is key to ensuring that models are accurate, original, and trusted. Relying on third-party data—or information obtained from external sources—to train AI tools makes it difficult to ensure that output is accurate.

For example, data brokers may have old data, incorrectly combine data from devices or accounts that don't belong to the same person, or make inaccurate inferences based on the data. This applies for our customers when we are grounding the models in their data. If the data in a customer's CRM all came from data brokers, the personalization may be wrong.

Keep data fresh and well labeled

AI is only as good as the data it's trained on. Models that generate responses to customer support queries will produce inaccurate or out-of-date results if the content it's grounded in is old, incomplete, and inaccurate, leading to "hallucinations" and stating falsehood as fact. Training data that contains bias will result in tools that propagate bias.

Companies must review all datasets and documents that will be used to train models and remove biased, toxic, and false elements. This process of curation is key to principles of safety and accuracy.

Ensure there's a human in the loop

Just because something can be automated doesn't mean it should be. Generative AI tools aren't always capable of understanding emotional or business context or knowing when they're wrong or damaging.

Humans need to be involved to review outputs for accuracy, suss out bias, and ensure models are operating as intended. More broadly, generative AI should be seen as a way to augment human capabilities and empower communities, not replace or displace them.

Companies play a critical role in responsibly adopting generative AI and integrating these tools in ways that enhance, not diminish, the working experience of their employees and their customers. This comes back to ensuring the responsible use of AI in maintaining accuracy, safety, honesty, empowerment, and sustainability; mitigating risks; and eliminating biased outcomes. And the commitment should extend beyond immediate corporate interests, encompassing broader societal responsibilities and ethical AI practices.

Test, test, test

Generative AI cannot operate on a set-it-and-forget-it basis—the tools need constant oversight. Companies can start by looking for ways to automate the review process by collecting metadata on AI systems and developing standard mitigations for specific risks.

Ultimately, humans also need to be involved in checking output for accuracy, bias, and hallucinations. Companies can consider investing in ethical AI training for front-line engineers and managers so they're prepared to assess AI tools. If resources are constrained, they can prioritize testing models that have the most potential to cause harm.

Get feedback

Listening to employees, trusted advisers, and impacted communities is key to identifying risks and course-correcting. Companies can create a variety of pathways for employees to report concerns, such as an anonymous hotline, a mailing list, a dedicated Slack or social media channel, or focus groups. Creating incentives for employees to report issues can also be effective.

Some organizations have formed ethics advisory councils—composed of employees from across the company, external experts, or a mix of both—to weigh in on AI development. Finally, having open lines of communication with community stakeholders is key to avoiding unintended consequences.

. . .

With generative AI going mainstream, enterprises have the responsibility to ensure that they're using this technology ethically and mitigating potential harm. By committing to guidelines and constructing guardrails in advance, companies can ensure that the tools they deploy are accurate, safe, and trusted—and that they help humans flourish.

Generative AI is evolving quickly, so the concrete steps businesses need to take will evolve over time. But sticking to a firm ethical framework can help organizations navigate this period of rapid transformation.

TAKEAWAYS

The adoption of generative AI by businesses comes with ethical risk. To be mindful of these risks and to take necessary steps to reduce them, organizations must prioritize the responsible use of generative AI by ensuring it is accurate, safe, honest, empowering, and sustainable.

- ✓ Human oversight and participation in decision-making processes should be actively encouraged to ensure that generative AI is used responsibly.

- ✓ Transparency, fairness, responsibility, accountability, and reliability are the trusted AI principles announced by Salesforce. These principles are applicable to any company making an AI investment.

✓ Strategies for responsibly integrating generative AI and reducing ethical risk include using first-party or zero-party data, maintaining updated and well-labeled data, involving humans in the process, iteratively testing models, and soliciting input from internal and external advisers.

NOTES

1. "IT Leaders Call Generative AI a 'Game Changer' but Seek Progress on Ethics and Trust," salesforce.com, March 6, 2023, https://www.salesforce.com/news/stories/generative-ai-research/.

2. "Salesforce Debuts AI Ethics Model: How Ethical Practices Further Responsible Artificial Intelligence," salesforce.com, September 2, 2021, https://www.salesforce.com/news/stories/salesforce-debuts-ai-ethics-model-how-ethical-practices-further-responsible-artificial-intelligence/.

3. Saul and Dina Bass, "Artificial Intelligence Is Booming—So Is Its Carbon Footprint," *Bloomberg*, March 9, 2023, https://www.bloomberg.com/news/articles/2023-03-09/how-much-energy-do-ai-and-chatgpt-use-no-one-knows-for-sure; Nabiha Syed, "The Secret Water Footprint of AI Technology: A Conversation with Shaolei Ren," The Markup, April 15, 2023, https://themarkup.org/hello-world/2023/04/15/the-secret-water-footprint-of-ai-technology.

Adapted from content posted on hbr.org, June 5, 2023 (product #H07OC4).

THE AI HYPE CYCLE IS DISTRACTING COMPANIES

by Eric Siegel

You might think that news of "major AI break-throughs" would do nothing but help machine learning's (ML) adoption. If only. Even before the latest splashes—most notably OpenAI's ChatGPT and other generative AI tools—the rich narrative about an emerging, all-powerful AI was already a growing problem for applied ML. That's because for most ML projects, the buzzword *AI* goes too far. It overly inflates expectations and distracts from the precise way ML will improve business operations.

Most practical use cases of ML—designed to improve the efficiencies of existing business operations—innovate in fairly straightforward ways. Don't let the glare emanating from this glitzy technology obscure the simplicity of its fundamental duty: The purpose of ML is to issue actionable predictions, which is why it's sometimes also called *predictive analytics*. This means real value, as long as you eschew false hype that it is "highly accurate," like a digital crystal ball.

This capability translates into tangible value in an uncomplicated manner. The predictions drive millions of operational decisions. For example, by predicting which customers are most likely to cancel, a company can provide those customers incentives to stick around. And by predicting which credit-card transactions are fraudulent, a card processor can disallow them. It's practical ML use cases like those that deliver the greatest impact on existing business operations, and the advanced data science methods that such projects apply boil down to ML—and only ML.

Here's the problem: Most people conceive of ML as "AI." This is a reasonable misunderstanding. But "AI"

This article is a product of the author's work as the Bodily Bicentennial Professor in Analytics at University of Virginia Darden School of Business.

suffers from an unrelenting, incurable case of vagueness—it is a catch-all term of art that does not consistently refer to any particular method or value proposition. Calling ML tools "AI" oversells what most ML business deployments actually do. In fact, you couldn't overpromise more than you do when you call something "AI." The moniker invokes the notion of artificial general intelligence (AGI), software capable of any intellectual task humans can do.

This exacerbates a significant problem with ML projects: They often lack a keen focus on their value—exactly how ML will render business processes more effective. As a result, most ML projects fail to deliver value.[1] In contrast, ML projects that keep their concrete operational objective front and center stand a good chance of achieving that objective.

What Does "AI" Actually Mean?

> *"'AI-powered' is tech's meaningless equivalent of 'all natural.'"*
>
> —Devin Coldewey, *TechCrunch*, 2022

AI cannot get away from AGI for two reasons. First, the term is generally thrown around without clarifying whether we're talking about AGI or *narrow AI*, a term that essentially means practical, focused ML deployments. Despite the tremendous differences, the boundary between them blurs in common rhetoric and software sales materials.

Second, there's no satisfactory way to define AI besides AGI. Defining AI as something other than AGI has become a research challenge unto itself, albeit a quixotic one. If it doesn't mean AGI, it doesn't mean anything—other suggested definitions either fail to qualify as "intelligent" in the ambitious spirit implied by "AI" or fail to establish an objective goal. We face this conundrum whether trying to pinpoint (1) a definition for AI, (2) the criteria by which a computer would qualify as "intelligent," or (3) a performance benchmark that would certify true AI. These three are one and the same.

The problem is with the word *intelligence* itself. When used to describe a machine, it's relentlessly nebulous. That's bad news if AI is meant to be a legitimate field. Engineering can't pursue an imprecise goal. If you can't define it, you can't build it. To develop an apparatus, you must be able to measure how good it is—how well it performs and how close you are to the goal—so that you know you're making progress and so that you ultimately know when you've succeeded in developing it.

In a vain attempt to fend off this dilemma, the industry continually performs an awkward dance of AI definitions that I call *the AI shuffle*. AI means computers that do something smart (a circular definition). No, it's intelligence demonstrated by machines (even more circular, if that's possible). Rather, it's a system that employs certain advanced methodologies, such as ML, natural language processing, rule-based systems, speech recognition, computer vision, or other techniques that operate probabilistically (clearly, employing one or more of these methods doesn't automatically qualify a system as intelligent).

But surely a machine would qualify as intelligent if it seemed sufficiently humanlike, if you couldn't distinguish it from a human, say, by interrogating it in a chatroom—the famous *Turing test*. But the ability to fool people is an arbitrary, moving target, since human subjects become wiser to the trickery over time. Any given system will only pass the test at most once—fool us twice, shame on humanity. Another reason that passing the Turing test misses the mark is because there's limited value or utility in fooling people. If AI could exist, certainly it's supposed to be useful.

What if we define AI by what it's capable of? For example, if we define AI as software that can perform a task so difficult that it traditionally requires a human, such as driving a car, mastering chess, or recognizing human faces. It turns out that this definition doesn't work either because, once a computer can do something, we tend to trivialize it. After all, computers can manage only mechanical tasks that are well understood and well specified. Once the challenge is surmounted, the accomplishment suddenly loses its charm and the computer that can do it doesn't seem "intelligent" after all—at least not to the wholehearted extent intended by the term *AI*. Once computers mastered chess, there was little feeling that we'd "solved" AI.

This paradox, known as the *AI effect*, tells us that if it's possible, it's not intelligent. Suffering from an ever-elusive objective, AI inadvertently equates to "getting computers to do things too difficult for computers to do"—artificial impossibility. No destination will satisfy once you arrive; AI categorically defies definition. With due irony, the computer science pioneer Larry Tesler famously suggested that we might as well define AI as "whatever machines haven't done yet."

Ironically, it was ML's measurable success that hyped up AI in the first place. After all, improving measurable performance is *supervised machine learning* in a nutshell. The feedback from evaluating the system against a benchmark—such as a sample of labeled data—guides its next improvement. By this process, ML delivers unprecedented value in countless ways. It has earned its title as "the most important general-purpose technology of our era," as Andrew McAfee and Erik Brynjolfsson put it.[2] More than anything else, ML's proven leaps and bounds have fueled AI hype.

All In with Artificial General Intelligence

"I predict we will see the third AI winter within the next five years. . . . When I graduated with my PhD in AI and ML in '91, AI was literally a bad word. No company would consider hiring somebody who was in AI."

—Usama Fayyad, June 23, 2022, speaking at
Machine Learning Week

There is one way to overcome this definition dilemma: Go all in and define "AI" as AGI, software capable of any intellectual task humans can do. If this science fiction–sounding goal were achieved, I submit that there would be a strong argument that it qualified as "intelligent." And it's a measurable goal—at least in principle, if not in practicality. For example, its developers could benchmark the system against a set of 1 million tasks, including tens of thousands of complicated email requests you might send to a virtual assistant, various instructions for a warehouse employee you'd just as well issue to a robot, and even brief one-paragraph overviews for how the machine should, in the role of CEO, run a *Fortune* 500 company to profitability.

AGI may set a clear-cut objective, but it's out of this world—as unwieldy an ambition as there can be. Nobody knows if and when it could be achieved.

Therein lies the problem for typical ML projects. By calling them "AI," we convey that they sit on the same spectrum as AGI, that they're built on technology that is actively inching along in that direction. "AI" haunts ML. It invokes a grandiose narrative and pumps up expectations, selling real technology in unrealistic terms. This confuses decision-makers and dead-end projects left and right.

It's understandable that so many would want to claim a piece of the AI pie, if it's made of the same ingredients as AGI. The wish fulfillment AGI promises—a kind of ultimate power—is so seductive that it's nearly irresistible.

But there's a better way forward, one that's realistic and that I would argue is already exciting enough: running major operations—the main things we do as organizations—more effectively! Most commercial ML projects aim to do just that. For them to succeed at a higher rate, we've got to come down to earth. If your aim is to deliver operational value, don't buy "AI" and don't sell "AI." Say what you mean and mean what you say. If a technology consists of ML, let's call it that.

Reports of the human mind's looming obsolescence have been greatly exaggerated, which means another era of AI disillusionment is nigh. And, in the long run, we will continue to experience AI winters as long as we continue to hyperbolically apply the term *AI*. But if we tone down the rhetoric—or otherwise differentiate ML from AI—we will properly insulate ML as an industry from the next AI winter. This includes resisting the temptation to ride hype waves and refrain from passively affirming starry-eyed decision-makers who appear to be bowing at the altar of an all-capable AI. Otherwise, the danger is clear and present: When the hype fades, the overselling is debunked, and winter arrives, much of ML's true value proposition will be unnecessarily disposed of along with the myths, like the baby with the bathwater.

TAKEAWAYS

With breathtaking new capabilities from generative AI released every several months—and AI hype escalating at an even higher rate—it's high time we differentiate most of today's practical machine learning (ML) projects from generative AI's advances.

✓ For most ML projects, the term *AI* goes entirely too far. It alludes to human-level capabilities that are better described as AGI (artificial general intelligence)—software capable of any intellectual task humans can do—and no one knows if and when AGI could ever be achieved.

✓ In fact, ML initiatives are most effective when used to optimize existing processes; these are the types of solutions that provide the greatest return on investment for businesses.

✓ Including all ML initiatives under the "AI" umbrella oversells and misleads, contributing to a high failure rate for ML business deployments.

NOTES

1. Eric Siegel, "Models Are Rarely Deployed: An Industry-Wide Failure in Machine Learning Leadership," KD Nuggets, January 17, 2022, https://www.kdnuggets.com/2022/01/models-rarely-deployed-industrywide-failure-machine-learning-leadership.html.

2. Erik Brynjolfsson and Andrew McAfee, "The Business of Artificial Intelligence," hbr.org, July 18, 2017, https://hbr.org/2017/07/the-business-of-artificial-intelligence.

Adapted from content posted on hbr.org, June 2, 2023 (product #H07NQA).

About the Contributors

MARK ABRAHAM is a managing director and a senior partner at Boston Consulting Group.

OGUZ A. ACAR is a chair in marketing at King's Business School, King's College London.

GIL APPEL is an assistant professor of marketing at the George Washington University School of Business. His research uncovers insights driven by consumer interactions with digital technologies, such as big data, social media, NFTs, and AI.

KATHY BAXTER is the principal architect of ethical AI practice at Salesforce, developing research-informed best practices to educate Salesforce employees, customers, and the industry on the development of responsible AI. She collaborates and partners with external AI and ethics experts to continuously evolve Salesforce policies, practices, and products. She is a member of Singapore's Advisory Council on the Ethical Use of AI and Data and a

Visiting AI Fellow at NIST and is on the board of Equa-lAI. Prior to Salesforce, she worked at Google, eBay, and Oracle in user experience research. She is a coauthor of *Understanding Your Users: A Practical Guide to User Research Methodologies.*

NICOLA MORINI BIANZINO is the EY global CTO, focused on bringing technology products to EY clients, positioning technology at the heart of the organization, advising global clients on technology investment and their innovation agendas, and providing industrialized technology products to meet their most pressing business needs. An early AI pioneer, he wrote a thesis on the application of neural networks to business in 1997. He holds a master's degree in artificial intelligence and economics from the University of Florence.

DAVID DE CREMER is the Dunton Family Dean of D'Amore McKim School of Business and professor of management at Northeastern University (U.S.). Before moving to Northeastern University, he was the KPMG chaired professor in management studies at Cambridge University (U.K.) and a provost chaired professor in management and organizations at NUS Business School (Singapore), where he was also the founder and director of the Centre on AI Technology for Humankind. He is a

Thinkers50 Radar thought leader, included in the top 2% of scientists worldwide, and a Top 30 Global Management Speaker. He is the author of *The AI-Savvy Leader* (Harvard Business Review Press, 2024). His website is www.daviddecremer.com.

TOJIN T. EAPEN is an assistant professor at the Robert J. Trulaske Sr. College of Business at the University of Missouri and a principal consultant at Innomantra.

DAVID C. EDELMAN is an executive adviser and a senior lecturer at Harvard Business School.

BEN FALK is a director in EY's Chief Technology Office, helping lead EY's Emerging Technology Lab. He has a background in finance and technology, having spent a decade working for large hedge funds as an economist and strategist before joining an AI fintech startup leveraging natural language techniques. Before joining EY, he launched a personal data agency startup, helping consumers manage and enforce their personal data rights.

DANIEL J. FINKENSTADT is an assistant professor of defense management at the Naval Postgraduate School in Monterey, California, and a principal of the advisory firm Wolf Stake Consulting.

JOSH FOLK is a cofounder and the president of enterprise solutions at IdeaScale, a cloud-based innovation-software platform.

DINKAR JAIN is a visiting professor at the University of California Anderson School of Management, Los Angeles, and Santa Clara University. He is Meta's former head of artificial intelligence for ads and director of product management.

SHEEN S. LEVINE is an assistant professor at the University of Texas, Dallas, and Columbia University, New York, studying and teaching how people behave and how they impact others, organizations, and markets. He is thankful for the advice of Apollinaria Nemkova, AI PhD researcher.

SALLY E. LORIMER is a principal at ZS, a global professional services firm.

JULIANA NEELBAUER is a partner at Fox Rothschild in the corporate, intellectual property, emerging markets, and entertainment and sports law groups. She is a lecturer at the University of Maryland and Georgetown University regarding securities law, negotiations, digital assets, and business law.

TSEDAL NEELEY is the Naylor Fitzhugh Professor of Business Administration and senior associate dean of faculty and research at Harvard Business School. She is the coauthor of *The Digital Mindset: What It Really Takes to Thrive in the Age of Data, Algorithms, and AI* and the author of *Remote Work Revolution: Succeeding from Anywhere.*

MARC RAMOS is the chief learning officer of Cornerstone, a leader in learning and talent management technologies. Marc's career as a learning leader extends 25 years of experience with Google, Microsoft, Accenture, and Oracle.

YOAV SCHLESINGER is an architect of ethical AI practice at Salesforce, helping the company embed and instantiate ethical product practices to maximize the societal benefits of AI. Prior to coming to Salesforce, Yoav was a founding member of the Tech and Society Solutions Lab at Omidyar Network, where he launched the Responsible Computer Science Challenge and helped develop EthicalOS, a risk mitigation tool kit for product managers.

DAVID A. SCHWEIDEL is the Rebecca Cheney McGreevy Endowed Chair and Professor of Marketing at Emory University's Goizueta Business School. His research focuses on consumer interactions with technology and how this shapes marketing practice.

ARUN SHASTRI leads the artificial intelligence practice at ZS, a global professional services firm.

ERIC SIEGEL is a leading consultant and former Columbia University professor who helps companies deploy machine learning. He is the founder of the long-running Machine Learning Week conference series, a frequent keynote speaker, and executive editor of the *Machine Learning Times*. Eric authored the book *The AI Playbook: Mastering the Rare Art of Machine Learning Deployment* and the bestselling *Predictive Analytics: The Power to Predict Who Will Click, Buy, Lie, or Die*, which has been used in courses at hundreds of universities. He won the Distinguished Faculty Award when he was a professor at Columbia University, where he taught the graduate courses in machine learning and AI. Later, he served as a business school professor at University of Virginia Darden School of Business. Eric also publishes op-eds on analytics and social justice.

PRABHAKANT SINHA is a cofounder of ZS, a global professional services firm. He also teaches sales executives at the Indian School of Business.

LOKESH VENKATASWAMY is the CEO and managing director of Innomantra, an innovation and intellectual property consulting firm in Bengaluru, India.

MARC ZAO-SANDERS is the CEO and cofounder of filtered.com, which develops algorithmic technology to make sense of corporate skills and learning content.

Index

Is Your Business Ready for the Future?

If you enjoyed this book and want more on today's pressing business topics, turn to other books in the **Insights You Need** series from *Harvard Business Review*. Featuring HBR's latest thinking on topics critical to your company's success—from Blockchain and Cybersecurity to AI and Agile—each book will help you explore these trends and how they will impact you and your business in the future.